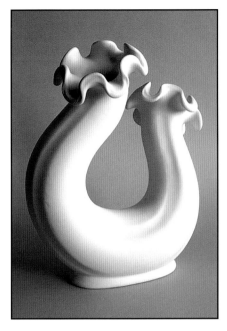

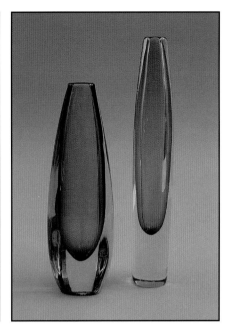

SCANDINAVIAN

CERAMICS & GLASS:

1940s to 1980s

George Fischler & Barrett Gould

Schiffer Publishing Ltd®

4880 Lower Valley Road, Atglen, PA 19310 USA

Dedication

This book is dedicated to Michelle and Aline, and especially to Peter who thought we would never finish.

Library of Congress Cataloging-in-Publication Data

Fischler, George.
Scandinavian ceramics & glass : 1940s to 1980s / George Fischler &
Barrett Gould.
p. cm.
ISBN 0-7643-1163-8 (hardcover)
1. Pottery, Scandinavian--Collectors and collecting--Catalogs. 2.
Pottery--20th century--Scandivania--Catalogs. 3. Glassware--
Scandinavia--Collectors and collecting--Catalogs. 4. Glassware--
Scandinavia--History--20th century--Catalogs. I. Gould, Barrett. II.
Title.
NK4113.F58 2000
738'.0948'075--dc21
00-009077

Cover design by Bruce Waters
Book design by Blair Loughrey
Type set in Zurich/Korinna

ISBN: 0-7643-1163-8
Printed in China
1 2 3 4

Published by Schiffer Publishing Ltd.
4880 Lower Valley Road
Atglen, PA 19310
Phone: (610) 593-1777; Fax: (610) 593-2002
E-mail: Schifferbk@aol.com
Please visit our web site catalog at
WWW.SCHIFFERBOOKS.COM

This book may be purchased from the publisher.
Include $3.95 for shipping.
Please try your bookstore first.
We are interested in hearing from authors
with book ideas on related subjects.
You may write for a free catalog.

In Europe, Schiffer books are distributed by
Bushwood Books
6 Marksbury Ave.
Kew Gardens
Surrey TW9 4JF England
Phone: 44 (0) 208 392-8585; Fax: 44 (0) 208 392-9876
E-mail: Bushwd@aol.com
Free postage in the U.K., Europe; air mail at cost.

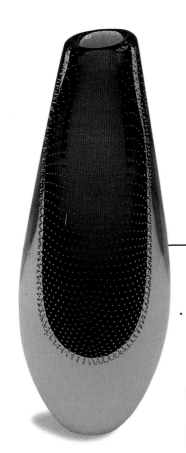

Contents

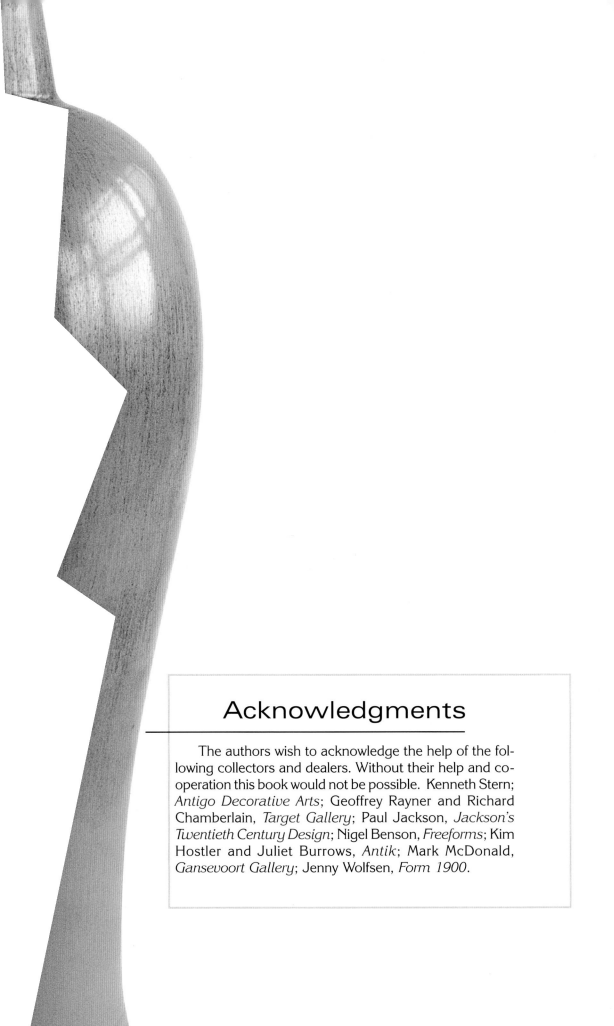

Acknowledgments

The authors wish to acknowledge the help of the following collectors and dealers. Without their help and cooperation this book would not be possible. Kenneth Stern; *Antigo Decorative Arts*; Geoffrey Rayner and Richard Chamberlain, *Target Gallery*; Paul Jackson, *Jackson's Twentieth Century Design*; Nigel Benson, *Freeforms*; Kim Hostler and Juliet Burrows, *Antik*; Mark McDonald, *Gansevoort Gallery*; Jenny Wolfsen, *Form 1900*.

Introduction

Scandinavia is the commonly used term when referring to the Nordic countries of Sweden, Denmark, Norway, Iceland and Finland. These countries all have long intertwined histories, sharing origins, language (except Finland) and political connections. While the history and tradition of ceramics and glass making date back to the eighteenth century, we will concern ourselves in this book with the period following the Second World War, with occasional excursions back to the 1920s.

Whenever Scandinavian design is discussed, there are several common threads. The relationship of the design to nature, function, quality, and individual craftsmanship predominate the discussion. The ultimate use of the individual pieces and their relationship to the consumer is always considered. In Demark and Sweden the use of subtle form, and in ceramics, glazes draw our attention. In Finland the forms of nature, particularly the forests and archipelagos of the many islands play a dominant role in the design. Linking all of these styles is a shared inheritance of Nordic folklore and legend.

The fine arts also play a role in the development of the aesthetic of modern Scandinavian design. Many of the most influential designers graduated or studied at fine arts institutes or academies. This allowed them to bring an artist's eye to even the most utilitarian of wares.

The factories in Scandinavia nurtured this pool of artistic talent. Many of them had extensive art and design departments. Some of the larger firms, such as Gustavsberg and Orrefors, devoted entire portions of their factories to their studio artists like Berndt Friberg and Edvin Öhrström. The output from these artists was vigorously promoted through exhibitions including "Finlandia" in 1961, "Scandinavia at Table" in 1951, "Design in Scandinavia" in 1954, and "Svensk Form" in 1980. Recognition was also given to these artists, many of whom worked in glass, ceramics, and metal, by Frederik Lunning, who was the Georg Jensen distributor in New York. The Lunning Prize was awarded annually between 1951 and 1970 to promising artists.

This book will illustrate some of the glass and ceramics produced by a few of the many artists working in the post-war period, presenting a cross section of their work. The focus is primarily on the studio works and will give the reader a flavor for the post-war style that has come to be known as Scandinavian Modern.

Collecting and Valuing

As with any area of collecting, the actual value of a particular item is ultimately what someone is willing to pay at any given time or place. Values will vary by location and by desirability at a particular time. There are, however, some points to keep in mind. Never buy something just because it's "hot." People should collect because they like what they are buying. That said, it is also true that there are good ceramics and glass pieces, and common or mediocre pieces. Values for fine examples of unique, hand made items will always be higher than for mass produced pieces. Pieces which were hand thrown by individual artists naturally are limited in number, and cannot be duplicated. Most artists whose work is illustrated in this book produced both. That is not to say that just because something was mass-produced it is not good, just that it may not have the personality of the artist imprinted on it. There are also many studio pieces by quality artists that may not represent their best work.

The values listed in this book represent the authors opinions about the pieces illustrated for items without defects, and in no way should be used as the final authority on price. The authors assume no risk for profit or loss incurred from use of this guide.

Part I: Ceramics

Denmark

The oldest, and one of the two largest, ceramic factories in Denmark is Royal Copenhagen. Founded in 1755, the firm produced porcelain in the prevailing French style. It was not until the last quarter of the nineteenth century that artistic production became noteworthy. Arnold Krog, art director at Royal Copenhagen from 1885-1916, led the company to international recognition. Working with Japanese-inspired designs, the firm produced fine porcelain art-ware. At the turn of the century, exceptional crystalline glazes developed by his chemist, Valdemar Engelhardt, enhanced Krog's designs.

During the first quarter of the twentieth century, Royal Copenhagen also produced multicolored glazed stoneware by Patrick Nordström, who worked there from 1912-1922. Nordström had studied in Paris and developed distinctive glazes. From 1920-1940 production primarily consisted of porcelain figures, hand molded and decorated. Knud Kyhn and Jais Nielsen developed sculptural forms, which dominated the 1920s. During this time, Axel Salto and Nils Thorsson made art ware and tableware in the modern style. The most influential artist was probably Axel Salto. Salto started out working for Bing and Grøndahl from 1923-1925. Then he moved to Saxbo where he worked from 1925 to 1933. In 1933, he joined Royal Copenhagen. Salto designed a natural "budding and sprouting" style, inspired by plant forms. His highly incised and carved forms were mellowed with flowing earth-tone glazes. Nils Thorsson worked at Royal Copenhagen from 1912-1975 developing and design-

Top right: Royal Copenhagen, ca. 1940. Maroon glazed jug with figural design. Designed by Bode Willumsen. *Courtesy of Antigo Decorative Arts, London.* $450-650.

Left: Royal Copenhagen, ca. 1950. Beige and brown shaded matte glaze vase. *Courtesy of Antigo Decorative Arts.* $100-150.

  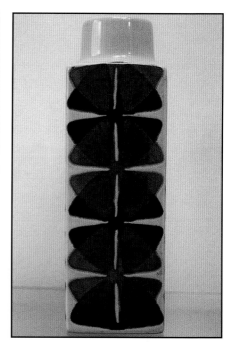

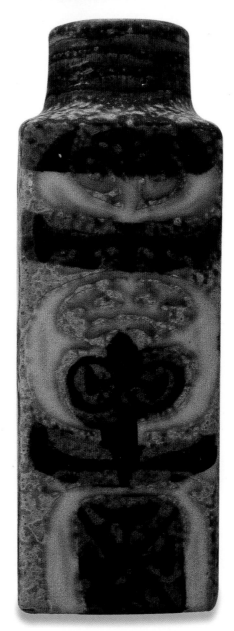

Royal Copenhagen, ca. 1970. Rectangular vases with abstract glaze decoration. Designed by Nils Thorsson. The pieces designed by Thorsson during the 1960s and 70s were some of Royal Copenhagen's most popular of the period. *Courtesy of Antigo Decorative Arts, London.* $100-200.

ing matte glazed, incised, decorated stoneware in various modern forms.

In the 1960s and 1970s Royal Copenhagen featured a group of artists/designers who produced modern stoneware, porcelain art ware and dinnerware. Among them were Grethe Meyer, Eva Stæhr-Nielsen, Anne-Marie Trolle and Gertrud Vasegaard. Gerthe Meyer designed a porcelain dinnerware set, "Blue Line," in the early 1960s. It was modern-styled in elegant white porcelain, minimally decorated with a thin blue stripe. Eva Stæhr-Nielsen worked at Royal Copenhagen from 1968-1976. Her work typically was glazed stoneware, often with incised decoration. Anne-Marie Trolle worked at Royal Copenhagen from 1966-1972. Her designs included a sophisticated porcelain dinnerware set called "Domino," that received several international design awards. Gertrud Vasegaard, previously an independent studio potter, worked at Royal Copenhagen from 1959-1975. During this time she produced fine stoneware. In 1975, Vasegaard designed a porcelain dinnerware service called "Capella" in a modern Japanese-influenced style. Though much of Royal Copenhagen's output consists of traditional figurines and giftware of high quality, the firm also had, and continues to have, talented and innovative artists working in modern and contemporary styles.

In 1986 the company purchased Georg Jensen, and, in 1987, they bought Bing and Grøndahl. In 1997 they merged with Orrefors, Kosta Boda, BodaNova and Venini, and have been re-named Royal Scandinavia.

Bing and Grøndahl was the second large ceramic concern in Denmark, established in 1853, in Copenhagen, by brothers M.H. and Harald Bing, and porcelain modeler, Frederik Grøndahl. Production consisted of porcelain art ware and dinnerware, usually highly decorated with enamel and gilt ornamentation. Jens Ferdinand Willumsen was art director at Bing and Grøndahl from 1897-1900. During this time he encouraged his artists and designers to be creative. Underglazed porcelain work, at times incorporating intricate openwork design, was popular. Although traditional porcelain continued to be a mainstay, Bing and Grøndahl produced stoneware beginning at the turn of the century. In the 1930s Bing and Grøndahl produced a modernist porcelain dinnerware set designed by Kay Bojesen, a multi-medium artist. In the decade after World War II the firm employed many talented artists who designed in a modernist style. Included among them were George Hetting, Henning Koppel, Erik Magnussen, Ebbe Sadolin, Gertrud Vasegaard, and Myre Vasegaard.

George Hetting, during the 1950s and 1960s, produced hand worked stoneware in carved relief, and oriental inspired designs with rich glazes.

Henning Koppel, a noted sculptor best known for his work in metal, jewelry, glass, and plastics, also worked with clay for Bing and Grøndahl from 1961-1981. In the early 1960s he designed innovative mod-

Top: Royal Copenhagen, ca. 1965. Small abstract decorated vase. Decorated by Nils Thorsson. $75-125.

Center: Royal Copenhagen, ca. 1970. Illustration of Nils Thorsson mark.

Bottom: Royal Copenhagen, ca. 1965. Two decorated faience bowls from the "Tenera" series designed by Inge-Lisa Koefoed. Designed in 1959 and still in production. $75-125.

Royal Copenhagen, ca. 1970. Two decorative wall plaques. $100-150

ern tableware in undecorated white porcelain. This color was known within the firm as "Koppel White."

Erik Magnussen, also a talented designer in multi media, has been working with Bing and Grøndahl since 1962. He designed stoneware and porcelain, some of it hand worked, but mainly he designed for production. Perhaps his most innovative ceramic design is a porcelain dinnerware set called "Form 25 Termo." Designed in 1965 it featured a teapot and cups without handles. They had an inner shell design that kept the hot contents away from the outer shell, allowing the user to handle it in comfort.

Ebbe Sadolin worked at Bing and Grøndahl from 1927, designing porcelain tableware in the 1930s as well as in the 1960s. He worked in a timeless functional style that belied Bauhaus roots.

Gertrud Vasegaard was with Bing and Grøndahl from 1949-1959, working with stoneware and porcelain in a traditional, often Orient-inspired style consisting of individual pieces as well as designs for mass production.

Myre Vasegaard, daughter of Gertrud, was at Bing and Grøndahl from 1955-1959. During this period she produced hand worked stoneware using various techniques.

In Denmark as in most of the other Scandinavian countries there existed many individual studio potters, such as Arne and Jacob Bang, most of whom worked for a major ceramic firm at one time or another. There were also many smaller ceramics companies. One of the smaller firms of note was the Saxbo factory, established 1929 in Denmark. Founded by Nathalie Krebs

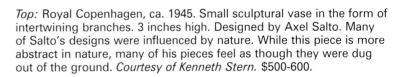

Top: Royal Copenhagen, ca. 1945. Small sculptural vase in the form of intertwining branches. 3 inches high. Designed by Axel Salto. Many of Salto's designs were influenced by nature. While this piece is more abstract in nature, many of his pieces feel as though they were dug out of the ground. *Courtesy of Kenneth Stern.* $500-600.

Center: Royal Copenhagen, ca. 1945. Olive green matte glaze vase with leafy decoration. 6 inches high. Designed by Axel Salto. *Courtesy of Kenneth Stern.* $800-1000.

Bottom: Royal Copenhagen, ca. 1945. Ivory and brown shaded budding vase. 6 inches high. Designed by Axel Salto. Some of Salto's most desirable pieces are in this so-called "budding" style. $650-800.

and Gunnar Nylund, the firm was so small that it shared some facilities with Bing and Grøndahl. The following year, Nylund left to join Rörstrand. Two years later, in 1932, Eva Stæhr-Nielsen joined the company. Together they produced fine quality matte glazed stoneware. Krebs developed orient-inspired glazes while Stæhr-Nielsen designed simple, yet bold, forms that won numerous international awards. In the 1950s a rustic, heavy, carved look was given to Saxbo stoneware production. Contributing to this change were designers Edith Sonne Bruun and Kirsten Weeke. In 1957 the company won a gold medal at the Milan Trienniale. Saxbo ceased production in 1968.

Another small firm is Nymølle, founded in 1936 by a retail company to produce inexpensive ceramics. It was not until mid 1940s that Nymølle produced quality ceramics. Nymølle's course was changed under the directorship of Jacob Bang, an established and talented studio potter who employed, among others, Gunnar Nyland, and Bjorn Wiinblad. Jacob Bang, in addition to being a potter, also was an architect, sculptor, and designer in glass and metals. His production ceramics for Nymølle featured simple, soft shapes with bright matte glazes, often bright blue or yellow. Bjorn Wiinblad, an artist working in various media including ceramics, joined Nymølle in 1946. Wiinblad's work reflects a style sometimes appearing cute or fussy. But his whimsical figurines and imaginative designs have made his name respected throughout much of the world. Gunnar Nyland, after many productive years at Rörstrand, joined Nymølle in 1959 and worked there until 1974. In 1976, the firm faced bankruptcy and closure, but was saved when Wiinblad purchased it.

Palshus was founded in 1947 by the husband and wife team of Per and Annelise Linnemann-Schmidt. For many years, the work of this firm was under-appreciated, and many collectors, even in Europe, did not value it highly. With the current interest in Scandinavian design, their work is receiving new and well-deserved attention. Strongly influenced by the designs of Saxbo, their early production consists of simple classical forms without decoration. The glazes, at their best, approach the work of such masters as Berndt Friberg. In the 1960s designs incorporating scrafitto decoration and rough primitive glazes on a chamotte clay body predominated. The firm ceased production in 1972. ∎

Saxbo, ca. 1934. Brown matte glaze jug with integral handle. 7 inches high. The handle has been formed by cutting the neck of the vase in half lengthwise, and then bending it down to form the handle. This early piece is one of Saxbo's best known designs. Designed by Nathalie Krebs, the founder of Saxbo. $500-600.

Above right: Saxbo ca. 1960. Rough brown volcanic glaze jug with integral handles. Designed by Edith Sonne Bruun. 8.5 inches high. *Courtesy of Antigo Decorative Arts, London.* $400-500.

Top left: Saxbo ca.1931. Mottled brown glaze narrow mouth vase. 8 inches high. This very early piece is incised on the bottom with the "flame" mark. This was changed in the early 1930s to the more familiar "yin & yang" mark, which was used until the end of production in 1968. *Courtesy of Antigo Decorative Arts, London.* $600-750.

Center left: Saxbo ca. 1960s. Blue-green matte glaze vase with incised medallion design. Designed by Eva Stæhr-Nielsen. *Courtesy of Antigo Decorative Arts, London.* $350-450.

Bottom left: Saxbo, ca. 1940. Blue glaze decorative plate with relief design. Designed by Jais Nielsen. *Courtesy of Antigo Decorative Arts, London.* $200-350.

Top left: Saxbo, ca. 1960s. Brown matte glaze narrow mouth vase with incised leaf design. Designed by Eva Stæhr-Nielsen. *Courtesy of Freeforms Ltd., London.* $350-450.

Top right: Saxbo, ca. 1960s. Brown matte glaze vase with incised line design. Designed by Eva Stæhr-Nielsen. *Courtesy of Freeforms Ltd., London.* $400-500.

Lower left: Saxbo, ca. 1950s. Elegant white matte glaze bottle form, narrow mouth vase. 4 inches high. Designed by Eva Stæhr-Nielsen. $275-375.

Bottom right: Saxbo, ca. 1960s. Brown matte glaze narrow mouth vase. Designed by Eva Stæhr-Nielsen. *Courtesy of Jackson's Twentieth Century Design, Stockholm.* $400-500.

Top left: Saxbo ca. 1960s. Brown glaze globular "artichoke" vase. *Courtesy of Antigo Decorative Arts, London.* $500-600

Top right: Saxbo, ca. 1960s. Brown matte glaze narrow long necked vase. 6 inches high. Designed by Eva Stæhr-Nielsen. $350-450

Left: Saxbo, ca. 1950s. Black, and white glaze bulb form vases. 4.75 inches high. These vases, designed by Stæhr-Nielsen, illustrate the high quality of the glazes produced by Krebs at Saxbo. While they do not achieve the ethereal quality of the best glazes produced by Bernt Friberg at Gustavsberg in Sweden, they have a serene tactile quality, similar to that made by Palshus. $350-450.

Top: Saxbo, ca. 1940s. Intense cobalt blue matte glaze vase. 5 in. diameter. The elegant intense blue color, combined with the simple bowl shape helps explain the popularity of Saxbo pottery. It's timeless. $400-500.

Lower left: Saxbo, ca. 1950s. Small eggplant color glaze spherical vase. 2.5 inches high. *Courtesy of Kenneth Stern.* $200-300.

Lower right: Saxbo, ca. 1950s. Small yellow matte glaze vase with inverted rim. 2.25 inches high. This soft yellow glaze is one of the more elegant glazes produced by Saxbo. *Courtesy of Kenneth Stern.* $250-350.

Top: Saxbo, ca. 1950s. White matte glaze vase. 3.5 inches high. *Courtesy of Kenneth Stern.* $200-300.

Center: Saxbo. Example of the "yin & yang" mark used by Saxbo from the early 1930s until the end of production in 1968. Eva Stæhr-Nielsen's initials (E.St.N) can be seen incised at the bottom.

Left: Palshus, ca. 1950. Blue matte glaze bowl. 4 inches high. Designed by Per Linnemann-Schmidt, marked PLS 1123. *Courtesy of Antigo Decorative Arts, London.* $400-500.

Top: Palshus, ca. 1950. Light blue matte glaze cylindrical vase. 5 inches high. Designed by Per Linnemann-Schmidt, marked PLS 1152. The pottery designed by the husband and wife team of Per and Annelise Linnemann-Schmidt is reminiscent of both Saxbo and the work of Berndt Friberg at Gustavsberg. The pieces they produced from the late 1940s to the mid-1960s consist of undecorated simple shapes. The glazes, particularly the blues are spectacular and subtle. $275-375.

Bottom: Palshus, ca. 1950. Light seafoam green matte glaze bowl. 5 in. diameter. Designed by Per Linnemann-Schmidt, marked PLS 1124. $150-250.

Top: Palshus, ca. 1950. Two vases, ivory/green and brown matte glaze. 4.75 and 3.25 inches high. Designed by Per Linnemann-Schmidt, marked PLS 402. $300-400.

Bottom: Palshus, ca. 1950. Brown matte glaze vase. 5 inches high. Designed by Per Linnemann-Schmidt. *Courtesy of Kenneth Stern.* $250-350.

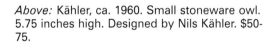

Above: Kähler, ca. 1960. Small stoneware owl. 5.75 inches high. Designed by Nils Kähler. $50-75.

Above center: Palshus, ca. 1965. Green mottled bottle-shape vase with incised sgraffito decoration. 6 inches high. Designed by Per Linnemann-Schmidt. Beginning in the mid-1950s, Palshus produced a less subtle style of pottery on a dark Chamotte body clay. These pieces were usually incised with designs or carved, the glazes no longer subtle. *Courtesy of Antigo Decorative Arts, London.* $250-350.

Above right: Palshus, ca. 1950. Example of the mark used on the early style pieces.

Two at right: Kähler, ca. 1960. Two small stoneware vases in blue and yellow glaze with incised decoration. 3 inches high. Designed by Nils Kähler. $75-125

Top: Kähler, ca. 1960. Green matte glaze dish. 5.5 in. diameter. Designed by Nils Kähler. $50-75

Lower left: Kähler, ca. 1960. Green matte glaze decorated flask. 7 inches high. Designed by Nils Kähler. $75-125

Lower right: Kähler, ca. 1960. Shopmark HAK.

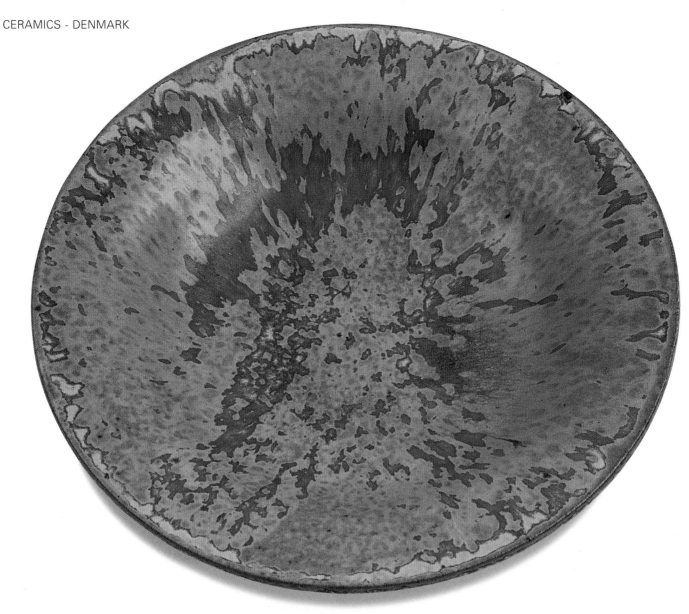

Top: Arne Bang, ca. 1950. Large charger in splotchy green and brown glaze. 11 in. diameter. In addition to creating ceramics with truly unusual textural glazes under his own name, Bang worked with his brother, Jacob Bang, at Holmegaard Glassworks. $400-600

Lower left: Arne Bang, ca. 1940. Volcanic earth tone glaze bowl with ribbed design. 4.5 in. diameter. $200-300.

Lower right: Signature mark of Arne Bang.

Top: Dansk, ca. 1965. Matte glazed creamer and sugar bowl. Designed by Jens Quistgaard. $50-75.

Bottom: Nymølle, ca. 1960. Mustard color high gloss glaze hourglass shaped vase, with underglaze decoration. Designed by Gunnar Nylund. *Courtesy of Antigo Decorative Arts, London.* $150-250.

23

Left: Nymølle, ca. 1960. Green glazed plate with incised leaf design. Designed by Gunnar Nylund. *Courtesy of Antigo Decorative Arts, London.* $75-150.

Right: Nymølle, ca. 1960. Chocolate brown semi-matte glaze pitcher. Designed by Gunnar Nylund. *Courtesy of Antigo Decorative Arts, London.* $200-300.

Top left: Nymølle, ca. 1950. Earthy blue glazed egg-shaped vase with sgraffito decoration. Designed by Jacob Bang. $200-300.

Top right: Nymølle, ca. 1950. Nymølle mark with the initials JB for Jacob Bang.

Bottom: Nymølle, ca. 1965. Decorated plate and cup. The design incorporating the word "Denmark." Designed by Bjorn Wiinblad. $50-75.

Top: Nymølle, ca. 1960. Slate blue semi-matte glaze spherically shaped vase. 4 inches high. Designed by Gunnar Nylund. *Courtesy of Kenneth Stern.* $175-275.

Lower left: Small squat vase in brown and yellow streaked glaze, ca. 1950. *Courtesy of Antigo Decorative Arts, London.* $100-150.

Lower right: Nymølle, ca. 1960. Partially glazed vase with incised underglaze decoration, the glossy red glaze and the unglazed body provide an interesting contrast. 3.75 inches high. Designed by Gunnar Nylund. *Courtesy of Kenneth Stern.* $200-300.

Left: Upswept design, blue/gray streaked matte glaze vase, ca. 1955. *Courtesy of Target Gallery, London.* $100-150.

Right: Partially glazed cylindrical vase, with impressed decoration, ca. 1970. $75-125.

Top left: Hand painted decorated bowl, ca. 1950. $50-100.

Top center: Thomas Toft, ca. 1965. Blue matte glazed bowl. $75-125

Top right: Knabstrup, ca. 1960. Blue glazed vase. $50-75.

Right: Dark brown semi-matte glaze vase, ca. 1950. Designed, glazed, and thrown by Jens Quistgaard. Prior to his association with Dansk, Quistgaard worked in both ceramics and wood. $150-250.

Left: Two small vases in brown and slate blue glaze, ca. 1950. 4.5 inches high. Designed by Rolf Palm. *Courtesy of Kenneth Stern.* $125-175.

Right: Olive brown matte glaze vase, ca. 1950. 4 inches high. Designed by A. Holm. *Courtesy of Kenneth Stern.* $400-500.

Three teapots, ca. 1960. Utilitarian wares such as tea pots, coffee pots, and dinnerware were all part of the overall Scandinavian design esthetic. The tradition of craftsmanship and style is evident in these pieces. $75-150.

Top: Blue glazed decorative plaque with fish, ca. 1970. $50-100.

Bottom left: Feline plate, ca. 1960. $25-50.

Bottom right: Yellow glazed button paperweight with leaf design, ca. 1960. $25-50.

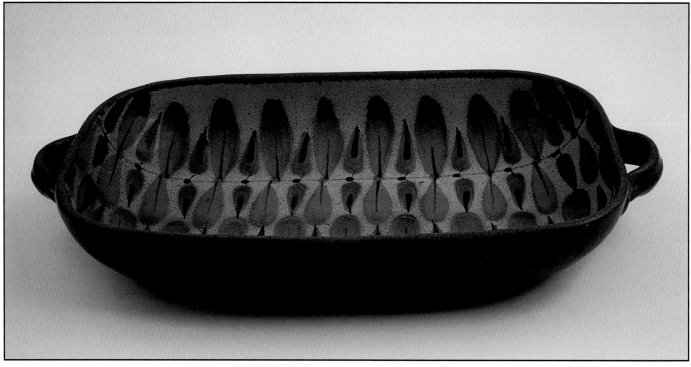

Two glazed decorated cooking
vessels, ca. 1965. $50-100.

Finland

By far the largest and most important ceramic concern in Finland was, and is, Arabia. Established in 1874 by the Swedish firm, Rörstrand, Arabia was formed to take advantage of lower import duties for Finnish trade to Russia. Arabia remained under Swedish ownership until 1916. Before 1916 Arabia produced ceramics similar to that of Rörstrand. Under Finnish ownership the firm expanded in new directions. Production ranged from bricks, tiles, and industrial ceramics, to production art and dinnerware. Individual studio efforts, in earthenware, porcelain, and stoneware were also produced. Beginning under the direction of Kurt Eckholm, who became artistic director in 1932, and throughout the 1970s Arabia produced interesting and innovative ceramics by artists that included Aune Siimes, Toini Muona, Friedl (Holzer) Kjellberg, Michael Schilkin, and Birger Kaipiainen. They were part of a core of award winning artists who created a foundation for post-war ceramics of quality and diverse design.

Aune Siimes, with Arabia from 1932-1964, produced fine translucent porcelain in soft shapes, using a slip cast technique to create a layered effect to the glaze.

Toini Muona worked at Arabia from 1931-1970. During this time she produced a range of nature-inspired stoneware and porcelain. Known mainly for her tall slender stoneware vases ranging from 15"-20" in height with exceptional glazes, Muona also made wall plaques and slab constructed pottery, maintaining a natural theme throughout.

Michael Schilkin, primarily a ceramic sculptor, produced carved relief wall plaques and three-dimensional

Top: Arabia, ca. 1965. Teapot in the "Ruska" pattern glaze on S design body. Designed by Ulla Procopé. The S design dinner service was first created in 1961 and is still in production with many glaze and decoration varieties. The "Ruska" glaze is one of the most popular. $75-125.

Bottom: Arabia, ca. 1967. Teapot, creamer, and sugarbowl in the "Kosmos" pattern on S design body. Designed by Ulla Procopé. $75-125.

33

Top: Arabia, ca. 1960. Ovenproof casserole pot in the "Leikki" (Flame) design. Designed by Ulla Procopé, and in production from 1958-1978. $100-150.

Center: Arabia, ca. 1955. Two teapots in the "GA" design. Designed by Ulla Procopé. $150-250.

Bottom: Arabia, ca. 1950. A vase and pitcher in black glaze with incised floral and fruit design. $125-175.

pieces for Arabia from 1936-1962. He chose animal motifs for most of his work, and in the 1950s his work became more stylized.

Birger Kaipiainen worked with Arabia from 1937-1954, returning in 1958 after four years with Rörstrand. Although he designed several dinnerware patterns for Arabia, Kaipiainen is best known for his wall plaques and sculptures, often incorporating birds or flower motif into his work. Kaipiainen's work is unique among Scandinavian artists. His three-dimensional bird sculptures were comprised of earthenware beads strung over wire forms, at times using small round mirror tiles or watch faces.

Friedl Kjellberg joined Arabia in 1924 and worked there until 1970. Kjellberg's designs for Arabia ranged from the utilitarian to individual studio ceramics. She may be best known for her Rice porcelain pieces. First designed in 1941, production was begun within four years. These pieces were difficult to make and required great skill. Small decorative holes were cut in the piece. These holes were then filled with the translucent glaze during firing. Production continued until 1974. It was produced again beginning in 1984. Kjellberg also designed pieces that were glazed with incredible blue barium glazes, usually with deep glaze pools in the bottom.

During the early post war years a new generation of artists joined Arabia bringing new ideas in different and varied directions. Among them were Kaj Franck, Rut Bryk, Oiva Toikka, Kyllikki Salmenhaara, Kaarina Aho, Ulla Procopé and Annikki Hovisaari.

Kaj Franck joined Arabia in 1945, becoming head of the houseware design department shortly thereafter. His designs for production dinnerware and art-ware in porcelain and stoneware became a mainstay for Arabia. The "Kilta" dinnerware set designed in 1948 was simple, modern, and stackable and set a standard for his design team to follow into the 1950s.

Rut Byrk was another innovative artist who worked for Arabia, starting in 1942. She designed and produced primarily wall plaques and wall tiles. The plaques often depicted people or animal scenes stylized in form and colored with dark colored glossy glaze. The tiles were incorporated into large wall plaques or even entire walls, often in complex geometric configurations.

Kyllikki Salmenhaara, primarily a studio potter, was at Arabia from 1947-1963, working with high-fired stoneware. Her stoneware work is rough textured, often brightly colored vases and bowls with sparse additional decoration, resulting in bold but graceful pots of excellent quality.

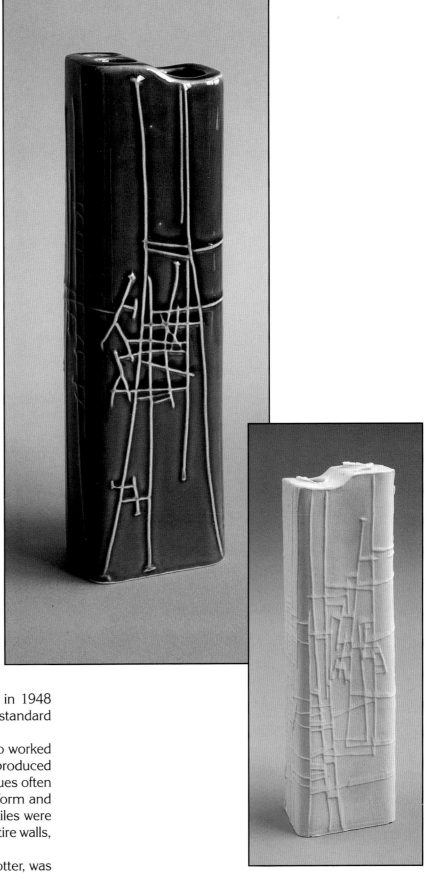

Arabia, ca. 1955. Two vases with abstract linear design. 8.5 inches high. Designed by Karl-Heinz Schultz-Koln. $275-375.

Arabia, ca. 1955. Pitchers
in the "FA" design body
with various decorations.
Designed by Kaj Franck.
$35-50.

As a member of Franck design team from 1946-1962 Kaarina Aho designed porcelain and stoneware dinnerware. She also designed some of the more whimsical ceramics that Arabia produced. Her egg dish, resembling a checkered hen on nest, and the fish shaped cutting board are classic Arabia production pieces.

Ulla Procopé also a member of Kaj Franck's design team at Arabia, from 1948-1967. During this time she designed several dinnerware lines for production. The most notable ones, "Ruska" and "Liekki," resembled hand thrown stoneware in simple shapes and earthy matte glazes.

Annikki Hovisaari, with Arabia from 1948-1974, worked with stoneware, hand thrown in modern and traditional designs. In the 1960s she also designed a production art-ware line called "Ornamentti." It featured a brightly colored modern geometric design made in stoneware and porcelain.

In the 1950s a new group of artists joined Arabia to help maintain the status of design into the 1970s. Among them were Raija Tuume, Richard Lindh, Francesca (Mascitti) Lindh, Liisa (Hallamaa) Larsen, and Gunvor Olin-Gronquist

Tuume worked at Arabia from 1959-1974. She produced hand thrown stoneware with coarse texture of high quality.

Liisa Hallamaa, with Arabia from 1950 to 1971, also produced stoneware in modern and traditional forms.

Gunvor Olin-Gronquist designed patterns for dinnerware production during the 1950s, later creating original ceramics that were organic in design.

Francesca Lindh added to Arabia's line with interesting stoneware of quality design, winning honorable mention at the 1957 Milan Trienniale.

Richard Lindh became head of the design department in 1973. In 1990 Arabia was taken over by Hackman, and in 1994 became part of the Designor Oy group.

A second and much smaller ceramic concern in Finland was Kupitaan Savi, first founded in the 18th century as a brickyard. It was not until the early 20th century that they produced art-ware and tableware (from 1915-1969). In the 1950s Kupitaan Savi's three leading artists, Linnea Lehtonen, Marjukka Paasivirta, and Okki Laine, created well-designed, often functional, stoneware of high quality. The company ceased production of ceramics in 1969.

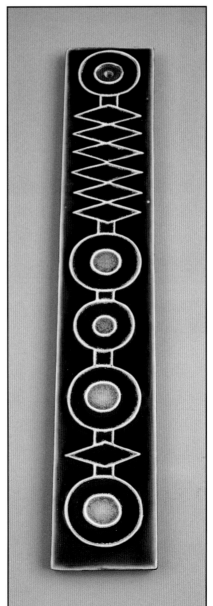

Top: Arabia, ca. 1970. Teapot with medallion design. Designed by Kaj Franck. $50-100.

Bottom: Arabia, ca. 1965. Decorative hanging plaque. 14.5 inches long. Designed by Annikki Hovisaari. $250-400.

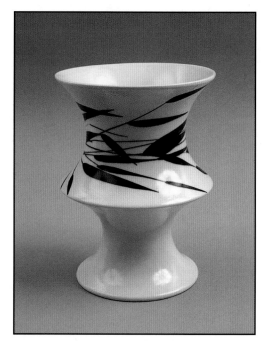

Top left & right: Arabia, ca. 1950. Bowls and vase in "Rice" porcelain. Designed by Friedl Kjellberg. The production of rice porcelain pieces was begun in 1941 and continued until 1974. This type of ceramic ware has its origins in 18th century China. It is difficult to produce and very delicate. The cut-outs in the body are filled only with the delicate glaze. New pieces were produced again by Arabia when production resumed after 1984. $250-600.

Above: Arabia, ca. 1960. Decorated platter. Decoration by Raija Uosikkinen. $50-75.

Right: Arabia, ca. 1960. White glazed vase with Japanese bamboo style decoration. $50-75.

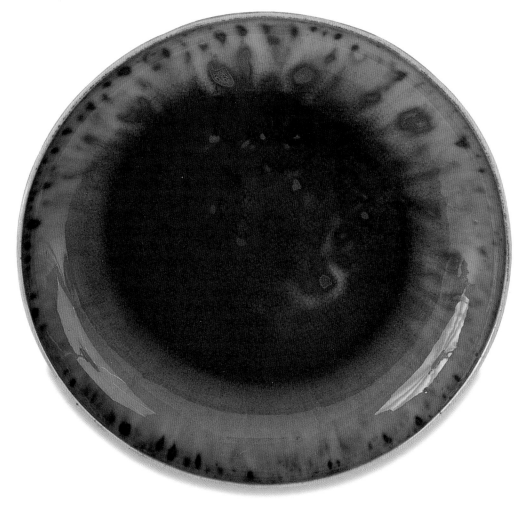

Top: Arabia, ca. 1965. Shallow bowl with internal barium glaze of intense blue. 5.75 in. diameter. Designed and glazed by Friedl Kjellberg. $400-500.

Bottom: Arabia, ca. 1965. Charger with pooled blue barium glaze. 10.75 in. diameter. Designed and glazed by Friedl Kjellberg. $900-1000

Top: Arabia, ca. 1960. Small high gloss glaze vase. 4 inches high. Designed by Annikki Hovisaari. $200-300.

Center: Arabia, ca. 1965. Light green matte glaze bowl. 4.5 in. diameter. Designed and glazed by Richard Lindh. *Courtesy of Kenneth Stern.* $350-450.

Bottom: Arabia, ca. 1960. Signature mark of Friedl Kjellberg. $350-450.

Sweden

Ceramic production in Sweden was dominated by the firms of Gustavsberg, Rörstrand, and Upsala-Ekeby. Most of the studio potters in Sweden worked for one or more of the big three at some point in their careers. Following a seemingly universal trend, a single conglomerate, Designor Oy, now owns all three companies.

The Gustavsberg factory was established in 1827 near Stockholm, on the site of another old ceramic factory. Production was limited to imitations of English wares throughout the 1800s. The history of the "modern" factory could be said to have begun in 1937, although it has earlier roots.

Wilhelm Kåge had begun his association with the firm in 1917 and was later to become art director, serving until 1949. Kåge led the production of fine quality ceramics with a unique combination of Art Deco and Classical style. Most familiar is the "Argenta" line, a matte green glazed stoneware with inlaid silver decoration. Although the green glaze is the most familiar, "Argenta" was also produced in white and brownish red glazes. Kåge also designed a line called "Surrea," which has a cubist, surrealistic quality, and "Cintra," porcelain so thin and delicate that you can almost read through it. Probably the most interesting work designed by Kåge, however, was the "Farsta" line. These individually designed, thrown and glazed pieces represent some of the most daring designs in Scandinavian studio pottery.

In the early 1940s, Berndt Friberg, hired by Wilhelm Kåge in 1934 as a thrower, began producing high quality stoneware with fine glazes in the Oriental style. Until his death in 1981, Friberg produced some of the most prized studio pottery in the world for Gustavsberg studio. While many great pottery artists worked in this period, none could match the combination of subtle form and glaze achieved by Friberg at his best. His work is the ultimate refinement of the Scandinavian "Sung" style.

Gustavsberg, ca. 1940. White "Surrea" sculpture. 10 inches high. Designed by Wilhelm Kåge. "Surrea" pieces, created by Kåge, feature both wildly surrealistic and cubist shapes. *Courtesy of Kenneth Stern.* $700-950.

Top left: Gustavsberg, ca. 1940. Small blue matte glaze vase. 3.75 inches high. Designed by Wilhelm Kåge. In addition to his studio pieces Kåge created some production pieces. This limited production piece is marked Kåge Verk Stad 195/300. $100-175.

Top right: Gustavsberg Studio, ca. 1945. Mustard yellow globular shaped "Farsta" vase. 4.25 inches high. Designed and made by Wilhelm Kåge. "Farsta" pieces were created by Kåge through the 1960s. They form one of the most intriguing series of studio-made pottery in Scandinavia. Kåge used unusual glazes, forms and incised designs in these pieces. *Courtesy of Kenneth Stern.* $500-600.

Bottom right: Gustavsberg Studio, ca. 1950. Blue high glaze bulbous form "Farsta" vase. 6.25 inches high. Designed and made by Wilhelm Kåge. *Courtesy of Kenneth Stern.* $650-750.

In 1937 Stig Lindberg joined Gustavsberg as a designer, he became art director in 1949 following Kåge. With the addition of Lindberg, the modern history of Gustavsberg began. Lindberg was one of the most prolific designers. He worked in many styles, beginning with the subtle classical look and progressing to a pure, almost pop, 1960s style. Lindberg used bright colors in bold designs and, often, bizarre patterns to create a new look for Gustavsberg's output.

Karin Björquist, a designer under Stig Lindberg was to become the next art director, during the 1960s and 1970s. She introduced several new tableware lines.

During the postwar period Gustavsberg employed other talented artists, among them, Anders Liljefors, and Lisa Larsen, each of them contributed in different ways. Anders Liljefors, working at Gustavsberg during the 1940s and 1950s, produced hand worked ceramic sculptures in a freeform manner using abstract form and dripping glazes. Sven Wejsfeldt has worked at Gustavsberg since the 1950's. In the 1970's he began producing pottery in the style of Friberg. Lisa Larsen brought a different dimension to Gustavsberg production by means of a series of whimsical ceramic animals and people that were retailed by Georg Jensen and other quality shops. Gustavsberg is now part of the conglomerate Designor Oy.

The Swedish Royal family established Rörstrand pottery near Stockholm in 1726. Bendt Reinholt Geiger bought it in 1797. During this time production consisted mainly of quality imitations of the prevailing English and French styles. In Sweden, Rörstrand's main competitor during this period was the Gustavsberg factory, which produced similar wares. This competitive situation continued into the twentieth century. Rörstrand like Gustavsberg employed some of the best artists and designers of the day, among them Edward Hald, Louise Adelberg, Carl-Harry Stålhane, Hertha Bengston, and Gunnar Nylund.

Edward Hald, primarily known for his glasswork as an artist and director for Orrefors, was also a freelance ceramist at Rörstrand from 1917-1927.

Louise Adelberg designed porcelain dinnerware in a conservative, yet lively, style known as Swedish Modern.

Carl-Harry Stålhane worked in stoneware, often tall and slender in form, with Chinese-style glazes, creating a unique combination of form and glaze.

Hertha Bengston was with Rörstrand from 1941-1964. During this time she designed tableware in porcelain for production as well as individual pieces in stoneware and porcelain. She is known for contrasting matte and glossy glazes on the same piece. Her best-known design is probably the "Blå Eld" (blue fire) dinnerware set designed in 1951.

Gunnar Nylund was head designer at Rörstrand from 1931 until the late 1950s, designing a full range of ceramics including stoneware animal figures and por-

Gustavsberg Studio, ca. 1955. Earthy blue/brown matte glaze long necked vase. 9 inches high. Designed and made by Wilhelm Kåge. *Courtesy of Kenneth Stern.* $1000-1200.

Gustavsberg Studio, ca. 1960. Three "Farsta" vases in earth tone matte glaze with sgraffito decoration. 3 to 8 inches high. Designed and made by Wilhelm Kåge. *Courtesy of Kenneth Stern.* $1000-2200.

celain dinnerware, as well as stoneware pieces highlighted with decorative glossy patterns contrasting with the buff stoneware background.

During the 1960s and 1970s Rörstrand's designers included Marianne Westman, Signe Persson-Melin, and Bertil Vallien, among others. In 1964, Rörstrand was purchased by Upsala-Ekeby. In 1983, they were purchased by Arabia, and in 1994 became part of Designor Oy, along with Gustavsberg and Iittala.

The third major ceramics manufacturer in Sweden was Upsala-Ekeby founded in 1886. In the twentieth century Upsala-Ekeby made dinnerware similar to that of Gustavsberg and Rörstrand, but without creative design innovations. Upsala-Ekeby production was basic and met the need for a lower priced market. Beginning in 1942 and continuing until 1962, Vicke Lindstrand was the art director. Later, under the direction of Marianne Westman, her staff also produced a line of art-ware consisting of vases and bowls often in single color glazes. Marie Simmulsen, Anna Lisa Thompson and other designers worked at Upsala-Ekeby. It is now part of Designor Oy.

Like Denmark, Sweden had small, often one or two person, companies producing studio ceramics. Tobo is probably the best-known small studio. Consisting of the husband and wife team of Erich and Ingrid Triller, the firm began producing stoneware in 1935. The hallmarks of Tobo were simple forms combined with simple, yet complex glazes. Unlike many other firms that would release pieces with slight imperfections, if a Tobo piece was not perfect it was destroyed. All their output consisted of hand thrown and glazed pieces. The firm ceased production with Erich's death in 1972. ■

Top: Gustavsberg, ca. 1945. "Argenta" flask and stopper with swimming fish design. 8.5 inches high. Designed by Wilhelm Kåge. "Argenta" stoneware was created by Kåge in 1930. It features silver inlays, in either figural or geometric designs, and was produced into the 1960s. *Courtesy of Kenneth Stern.* $500-750.

Bottom: Gustavsberg, ca. 1945. "Argenta" vase in "Surrea" form. 10 inches high. Designed by Wilhelm Kåge. $300-400.

Above left: Gustavsberg Studio, ca. 1945. Brown matte glaze vase. 4 inches high. Designed, glazed, and thrown by Berndt Friberg. Marked with the early BF Studio mark, this is one of Friberg's early pieces which clearly demonstrates his mastery of both form and glaze. *Courtesy of Kenneth Stern.* $650-800.

Top right: Gustavsberg, ca. 1950. "Argenta" plate with fish inlay on blood red glaze body. 7 inches in diameter. Designed by Wilhelm Kåge. Although most people know "Argenta" through the green glaze pieces, other colors were produced. *Courtesy of Kenneth Stern.* $250-350.

Bottom right: Gustavsberg, ca. 1955. "Argenta" vase on white matte glaze body. 8.75 inches high. Designed by Stig Lindberg. *Courtesy of Kenneth Stern.* $300-400.

Left: Gustavsberg Studio, ca. 1950. Brown hare fur matte glaze handled vase. 6 inches high. Designed, glazed, and thrown by Berndt Friberg. Although Friberg's pottery was always simple in design and almost never orna-mented, the use of handles, giving the pottery a classical look, was sometimes utilized. *Courtesy of Kenneth Stern.* $600-800.

Right: Gustavsberg Studio, ca. 1945. Brown matte glaze vase. 5 inches high. Designed, glazed, and thrown by Berndt Friberg. Marked with the BF Studio mark. *Courtesy of Kenneth Stern.* $350-500.

Gustavsberg
Studio, ca. 1945.
Ivory/blue matte
glaze handled vase.
8.25 inches high.
Designed, glazed,
and thrown by
Berndt Friberg.
Marked with the BF
Studio mark.
*Courtesy of
Kenneth Stern.*
$650-850.

Top left: Gustavsberg Studio, ca. 1960s. Blue matte glaze bowl and yellow matte glaze onion form vase. 4.75 in diameter and 3 inches high. Designed, glazed, and thrown by Berndt Friberg. $650-850.

Above right: Gustavsberg Studio, ca. 1965. Large blue matte glaze vase. 11.75 inches high. Designed, glazed, and thrown by Berndt Friberg. While most of the pieces Friberg produced were relatively small in size, he did produce larger works. These larger pieces, particularly those with matte glazes, provided an excellent canvas on which to see the depth and subtlety of the glaze. $5000-6000.

Center: Gustavsberg Studio, ca. 1945. Blue mottled matte glaze globular vase. 5.25 inches high. Designed, glazed, and thrown by Berndt Friberg. Marked with BF Studio mark. This is another early example of Friberg's work illustrating that, while it has a relatively thick body, it still achieves a delicate appearance. $1000-1200.

Bottom left: Gustavsberg Studio, ca. 1965. Blue matte glaze cylindrical bowl. 3 in. diameter. Designed, glazed, and thrown by Berndt Friberg. $350-450.

Gustavsberg Studio, ca. 1950s to 1960s. Several examples of footed matte glaze bowls produced by Friberg. The inspiration for the design of these bowls was taken from Chinese Sung Dynasty pieces. Using his mastery of both form and glaze, Friberg took the traditional tea bowl and created a unique, purely Scandinavian ceramic. *Courtesy of Kenneth Stern.* $250-500.

Gustavsberg Studio, ca. 1960. Two bowls in matte glaze, a yellow/rose and brown. 12 and 6 inch diameters. Designed, glazed, and thrown by Berndt Friberg. The pooling of the glaze at the bottom of these pieces creates another exciting design. *Courtesy of Kenneth Stern.* $350-600.

Top left: Gustavsberg Studio, ca. 1965. Yellow and green matte glaze vase with internal geometric glaze design. 9.25 inches high. Designed, glazed, and thrown by Berndt Friberg. During the 1960s Friberg experimented with the incorporation of subtle designs within the glaze. Extremely difficult to do well, this piece again provides an example of why Friberg is considered among the masters of the form. *Courtesy of Kenneth Stern.* $2200-2800.

Top right: Gustavsberg Studio, ca. 1952. Blue matte glaze classically shaped vase. 7 inches high. Designed, glazed, and thrown by Berndt Friberg. A good example of some of the subtle shadings which were achieved by Friberg. *Courtesy of Kenneth Stern.* $1200-1600.

Left: Gustavsberg Studio, ca. 1965. Two vases, one in white matte glaze, and the other a dark earthy green high gloss glaze. 3.5 and 4.5 inches high. Designed, glazed, and thrown by Berndt Friberg. *Courtesy of Target Gallery, London.* $450-650.

Top: Gustavsberg Studio, ca. 1960. Miniature bowls and vases. Under 2 inches in size. Designed, glazed, and thrown by Berndt Friberg. Many of the Scandinavian potters produced miniatures. *Courtesy of Kenneth Stern.* $500-900.

Bottom: Gustavsberg Studio, ca. 1966. Blue mottled high glaze bowl. 3 in. diameter. Designed, glazed, and thrown by Berndt Friberg. Beginning in the 1960s, Friberg began producing high glaze wares. While the glaze on these pieces is not as subtle as the matte glaze, it does allow more artistic expression. They are technically more difficult to produce and greatly expanded the palette of colors. *Courtesy of Kenneth Stern.* $350-500.

Top left: Gustavsberg Studio, ca. 1966. Green mottled high glaze vase. 7.5 inches high. Designed, glazed, and thrown by Berndt Friberg. $750-1000.

Top right: Gustavsberg Studio, ca. 1965. Two vases in high gloss oxblood glaze. 3 and 6.25 inches high. Designed, glazed, and thrown by Berndt Friberg. $450-650.

Bottom: Gustavsberg Studio, ca. 1965. Two blue mottled high glaze vases. 3.25 inches high. Designed, glazed, and thrown by Berndt Friberg. These Siamese twin vases illustrate the problems that can be encountered in the firing process. They still possess charm. *Courtesy of Kenneth Stern.*

Gustavsberg Studio, ca. 1965. High gloss glaze examples of the footed bowl design. Designed, glazed, and thrown by Berndt Friberg. *Courtesy of Kenneth Stern.* $350-600.

Top: Gustavsberg Studio, ca. 1970. Semi-matte glaze cylindrical vase. 20 inches high. Designed, glazed, and thrown by Berndt Friberg. This is one of the largest pieces made by Friberg. *Courtesy of Target Gallery, London.* $3000-4000.

Bottom: Gustavsberg Studio, ca. 1972. High gloss blue/violet aniara glaze vase and bowls. 2 to 3.5 inches high. Designed, glazed, and thrown by Berndt Friberg. The vase on the right is unusual in that it is octagonal, something of a challenge to produce on a wheel. The glaze colors vary from an intense sky blue to violet. $650-850.

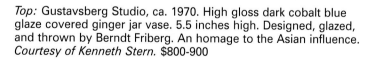

Top: Gustavsberg Studio, ca. 1970. High gloss dark cobalt blue glaze covered ginger jar vase. 5.5 inches high. Designed, glazed, and thrown by Berndt Friberg. An homage to the Asian influence. *Courtesy of Kenneth Stern.* $800-900

Center left: Gustavsberg Studio, ca. 1979. High gloss glaze white and green vase. 5 inches high. Designed, glazed, and thrown by Berndt Friberg. One of the last pieces made by Friberg. Beginning in 1975, pieces were dated rather than using a letter code. This piece illustrates Friberg's return to the pure Chinese form. $550-650.

Right: Gustavsberg, ca. 1955. Blue/green semi-matte glaze "Selecta" vase. 8.5 inches high. Although most collectors know Friberg for his individually thrown and glazed pieces, he did design pieces to be mass-produced. All hand thrown pieces are hand signed, the production pieces have paper labels. *Courtesy of Kenneth Stern.* $175-250.

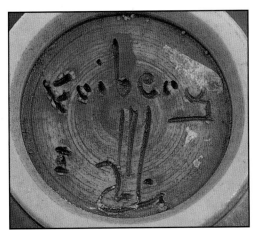

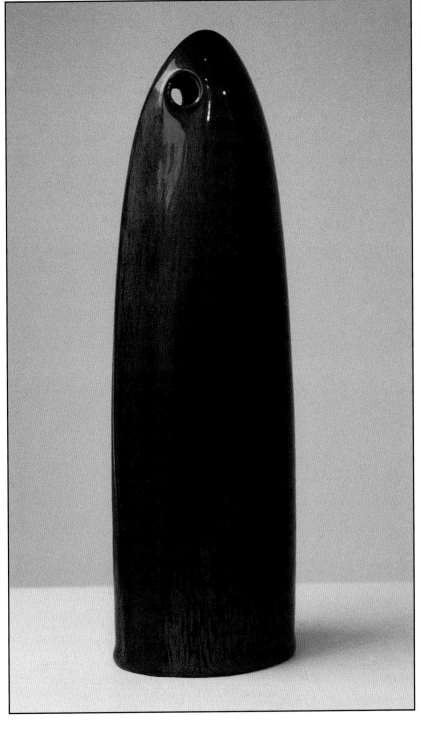

Top: Gustavsberg Studio, ca. 1967. Two examples of the Friberg mark found on the bottom of the Studio pieces. The Gustavsberg hand is incised along with the name Friberg, and a letter code for the date of production.

Above: Gustavsberg Studio, ca. 1945. Chamotte body figure in brown matte glaze. 12 inches high. Designed and made by Stig Lindberg. *Courtesy of Jackson's Twentieth Century Design, Stockholm.* $850-1000.

Left: Gustavsberg Studio, ca. 1950. Blue/brown hare fur semi-matte glaze sculpture. 9 inches high. Designed and made by Stig Lindberg. *Courtesy of Target Gallery, London.* $1000-1200.

Top left: Gustavsberg Studio, ca. 1950. Blue semi-matte glaze hyacinth vase. 10 inches high. Designed and thrown by Stig Lindberg. *Courtesy of Target Gallery, London.* $850-1000.

Top right: Gustavsberg Studio, ca. 1955. Brown/green mottled matte glaze hourglass-shape vase. 7.5 inches high. Designed and thrown by Stig Lindberg. *Courtesy of Target Gallery, London.* $500-600.

Bottom: Gustavsberg Studio, ca. 1960. Brown/cream semi-matte glaze bowl with impressed geometric design. 6.25 inch diameter. Designed and thrown by Stig Lindberg. This piece illustrates the combination of smooth surface with impressed repeating decoration favored by Lindberg in the 1960s. $300-400.

Gustavsberg Studio, ca. 1957. Commemorative tile in blue/green glaze. Designed and made by Stig Lindberg. *Courtesy of Target Gallery, London.* $300-400.

Gustavsberg Studio, ca. 1960. Three vases in brown/blue/green semi-matte glaze. Designed and thrown by Stig Lindberg. Lindberg produced stoneware with varying textures and innovative shapes. While he is well known for producing the same subtle and classic forms as Friberg, Nylund, and Stålhane, he also made some of the most interesting and unusual forms of Scandinavian ceramics of the mid-century. *Courtesy of Kenneth Stern and Jackson's Twentieth Century Design, Stockholm.* $500-1000.

Top left: Gustavsberg Studio, ca. 1962. Brown mottled textured semi-matte glaze vase with impressed design. 7.5 inches high. Designed and thrown by Stig Lindberg. In the 1960s the shapes produced by Lindberg combined the traditional vase shape with a more exciting contemporary hard-edged design. These pieces, produced in many colors, are uniquely Lindberg. $1500-2000.

Top right: Gustavsberg Studio, ca. 1960. Blue semi-matte glaze cylindrical vase. 7 inches high. Designed and thrown by Stig Lindberg. This is another example of Lindberg's break with traditional forms, by introducing and combining interesting design elements in a common shape. *Courtesy of Kenneth Stern.* $400-500.

Bottom: Gustavsberg Studio, ca. 1960. Mottled brown semi-matte glaze bottle form vase. 5 inches high. Designed and thrown by Stig Lindberg. *Courtesy of Kenneth Stern.* $300-400.

Top left: Gustavsberg Studio, ca. 1962. Blue/brown matte glaze, narrow mouth vase. 4 inches high. Designed and thrown by Stig Lindberg. *Courtesy of Kenneth Stern.* $250-350.

Top right: Gustavsberg Studio, ca. 1950. Beige/brown mottled semi-matte glaze vase with impressed design. Designed and thrown by Stig Lindberg. The design on this piece gives it a savage, primitive feel, and again shows Lindberg's range of expression. *Courtesy of Jackson's Twentieth Century Design, Stockholm.* $400-600.

Bottom: Gustavsberg Studio, ca. 1962. Blue/green semi-matte glaze vase with impressed geometric design. 9.75 inches high. Designed and thrown by Stig Lindberg. This wonderful example contrasts the depth and subtlety of the smooth glaze with the impressed design. $850-950.

Top left: Gustavsberg Studio, ca. 1962. Brown matte glaze miniature vase. 3.25 inches high. Designed and thrown by Stig Lindberg. The shape is reminiscent of Friberg, but the style is pure Lindberg. $300-400.

Top right: Gustavsberg Studio, ca. 1950. Blue shaded semi-matte glaze sculptural vase with impressed geometric design. 6 inches high. Designed and thrown by Stig Lindberg. The impressed design affects the progress of the glaze down the sides of this piece. *Courtesy of Kenneth Stern.* $500-600.

Bottom: Gustavsberg Studio, ca. 1960. Brown mottled gloss glaze, bulbous form vase. 7.5 inches high. Designed and thrown by Stig Lindberg. *Courtesy of Kenneth Stern.* $400-500.

Gustavsberg Studio, ca. 1962. Three cylindrical vases in brown glazes with impressed geometric designs. 6 to 7.5 inches high. Designed and thrown by Stig Lindberg. *Courtesy of Kenneth Stern.* $350-500.

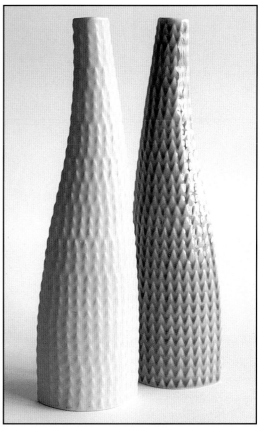

Gustavsberg, ca. 1965. Vases in the "Reptil" series. 5 and 9 inches high. Designed by Stig Lindberg. This series of tactile pieces, aptly named "Reptil," mimics reptile scales. *Courtesy of Jackson's Twentieth Century Design, Stockholm, and Kenneth Stern.* $250-350.

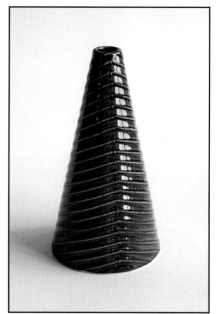

Left: Gustavsberg Studio, ca. 1960. Blue/green semi-matte glaze vase. 8 inches high. Designed and thrown by Stig Lindberg. *Courtesy of Kenneth Stern.* $600-800.

Top right: Gustavsberg, ca. 1965. "Domino" series vase in brown high gloss glaze. 5.25 inches high. Designed by Stig Lindberg. *Courtesy of Kenneth Stern.* $100-175.

Bottom right: Gustavsberg, ca. 1965. "Endiv" series vases in blue and black gloss glaze. Designed by Stig Lindberg. *Courtesy of Jackson's Twentieth Century Design, Stockholm.* $300-400.

Gustavsberg, ca. 1950. "Pungo" (pouch) series vases in black, and white glaze. Designed by Stig Lindberg. *Courtesy of Jackson's Twentieth Century Design, Stockholm.* $250-350.

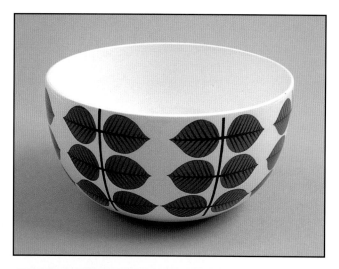

Top: Gustavsberg, ca. 1960. "Berså" series leaf design bowl. Designed by Stig Lindberg. In addition to designing and throwing studio pieces, Lindberg designed many utilitarian pottery wares. These were in production until 1974. The leaf series was only one of many. $35-50.

Center: Gustavsberg, ca. 1955. "Spisa-Ribb" series tableware. Designed by Stig Lindberg. $35-50

Bottom: Gustavsberg, ca. 1945. Hand painted faience plate. Designed by Stig Lindberg. Lindberg's association with hand painted faience pieces produced at Gustavsberg goes back to the 1940s. This relatively early piece shows the more whimsical designs typical of early work. $100-175.

Gustavsberg, ca. 1962. Hand painted faience platter. Designed by Stig Lindberg. $150-300.

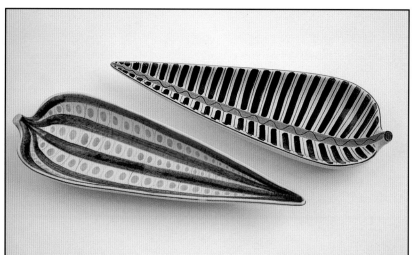

Gustavsberg, ca. 1960. Hand painted faience leaf
bowls. Designed by Stig Lindberg. Lindberg
produced a series of bowls shaped as leaves.
$100-200.

Gustavsberg, ca. 1955. Hand painted faience
handled pitchers. Designed by Stig Lindberg.
*Courtesy of Jackson's Twentieth Century
Design and Kenneth Stern.* $300-500.

Gustavsberg, ca. 1960. Hand painted faience combination candle holders and vases. Designed by Stig Lindberg. These pieces are reversible, one side will hold a candle, and when turned upside down is a vase. *Courtesy of Jackson's Twentieth Century Design, Stockholm, and Kenneth Stern.* $250-350.

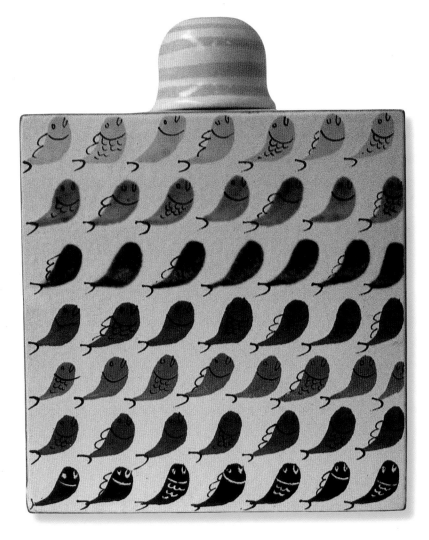

Top left: Gustavsberg, ca. 1960. Hand painted faience covered dish. Designed by Stig Lindberg. *Courtesy of Kenneth Stern.* $300-500.

Top right: Gustavsberg, ca. 1965. Mark found on handmade pieces of Stig Lindberg. They can be dated by looking at the placement of the name Stig L in relation to the Gustavsberg hand.

Center right: Gustavsberg, ca. 1946. Mark found on early studio pieces by Stig Lindberg. The letter denotes the date.

Bottom left: Gustavsberg, ca. 1962. Hand Painted faience "Spektra fisk" flask. Designed by Stig Lindberg. *Courtesy of Target Gallery, London.* $400-500.

Top: Gustavsberg, ca. 1964. "Afrika" series Tiger figurine. 10.25 inches long. Designed by Lisa Larson. Larson is best known for the series of figurines she produced from 1957 into the 1970s. Her earlier pieces, typical of those illustrated here display a charm that was not duplicated in her later work. $75-100.

Loer left: Gustavsberg, ca. 1964. "Afrika" series Lion figurine. 2 inches in diameter. Designed by Lisa Larson. $25-50.

Lower right: Gustavsberg, ca. 1958. "Stim" series fish plates. Designed by Lisa Larson. $25-50.

Top: Gustavsberg, ca. 1957. "Stora Zoo" series cat figurine.
Designed by Lisa Larson. $75-100.

Bottom: Gustavsberg, ca. 1958. "Beata" figurine. 5 inches high.
Designed by Lisa Larson. *Courtesy of Kenneth Stern.* $100-200.

Top: Gustavsberg Studio, ca. 1990. Intense yellow/green matte glaze dish. 7.25 inch in diameter. Designed, glazed, and thrown by Sven Wejsfeldt. $300-400

Center: Gustavsberg Studio, ca. 1986. Ivory matte glaze dish. 4.25 in. diameter. Designed, glazed, and thrown by Sven Wejsfeldt. Both the shape and glaze of this piece most closely approach the aesthetic ideals of the pieces done in the 1950s and 1960s at Gustavsberg. $250-350.

Bottom: Gustavsberg Studio, ca. 1989. Large bulbous vase with semi-matte glaze in shades of brown, violet and earth tones. 9.5 inches high. Designed, glazed, and thrown by Sven Wejsfeldt. The pieces produced by Wejsfeldt for the Gustavsberg studio are reminiscent of Friberg. $500-600.

Gustavsberg Studio, ca. 1991. Brown and blue/gray matte glaze long necked vase. 8 inches high. Designed, glazed, and thrown by Sven Wejsfeldt. *Courtesy of Kenneth Stern.* $400-500.

Above left: Gustavsberg Studio, ca. 1992. White mottled semi-matte glaze vase. 5.75 inches high. Designed, glazed, and thrown by Sven Wejsfeldt. *Courtesy of Kenneth Stern.* $350-500.

Above right: Gustavsberg Studio, ca. 1992. Bone/beige matte glaze long necked vase. 10.5 inches high. Designed, glazed, and thrown by Sven Wejsfeldt. *Courtesy of Kenneth Stern.* $400-600.

Bottom right: Gustavsberg Studio, ca. 1986. Mark of studio pieces by Sven Wejsfeldt.

Left: Gustavsberg, ca. 1950. Black glaze cylindrical vase with bubble design. 9.5 inches high. Designed by B.L. Sundell. *Courtesy of Kenneth Stern.* $350-450.

Right: Gustavsberg, ca. 1956. White and black textured glaze bulbous vase. 3 inches high. Designed by Anders Liljefors. *Courtesy of Kenneth Stern.* $150-250.

Top: Rörstrand, ca. 1940. Blue/black matte glaze ewer with ribbed glaze design. Designed by Gunnar Nylund. *Courtesy of Antigo Decorative Arts, London.* $250-400.

Above left: Rörstrand, ca. 1940. Celedon blue matte glaze classically proportioned vase. 6 inches high. Designed by Gunnar Nylund. *Courtesy of Kenneth Stern.* $450-600.

Bottom right: Rörstrand, ca. 1940. Mottled earthy brown matte glaze vase. 7.25 inches high. Designed by Gunnar Nylund. *Courtesy of Kenneth Stern.* $200-300.

Left: Rörstrand, ca. 1935. Brown semi-matte glaze vase. 10 inches high. Designed and made by Gunnar Nylund. Typical of early pieces, this one is marked NYLUND. *Courtesy of Kenneth Stern.* $650-850.

Right: Rörstrand, ca. 1940. Mottled chocolate brown bowl. 7.25 inches in diameter. Designed and made by Gunnar Nylund. $300-400.

Top: Rörstrand, ca. 1940. Brown matte glaze leaf shaped dish. 11.25 inches long. Designed and made by Gunnar Nylund. $100-200.

Bottom: Rörstrand, ca. 1940. Blue flecked ivory matte glaze vase with decoration. 7.5 inches high. Designed by Gunnar Nylund. Pieces designed and made by Nylund are marked either with the initials GN or the name Nylund. Pieces designed but possibly made or glazed by others at the factory bear two sets of initials. This piece is marked GN followed by AXI. It has been assumed that this second set of initials, also found on pieces by Stålhane, are those of the person who actually made them under Nylund or Stålhane's direction. This is more likely a glaze and shape code. *Courtesy of Kenneth Stern.* $200-300.

Top left: Rörstrand, ca. 1940. Brown matte glaze teapot. Designed by Gunnar Nylund. *Courtesy of Jackson's Twentieth Century Design, Stockholm.* $350-500.

Above right: Rörstrand, ca. 1950. Brown mottled matte glaze, nubby surface vase. Designed by Gunnar Nylund. $300-400.

Bottom left: Rörstrand, ca. 1940. Brown striated matte glaze "Rubus" vase. Designed and made by Gunnar Nylund. *Courtesy of Antigo Decorative Arts, London.* $150-250.

Rörstrand, ca. 1955. Five dishes and vase in a blue/
brown mottled glaze. Designed by Gunnar Nylund.
These dishes are typical of the biomorphic designs
produced by Nylund during the 1950s. $250-450.

Rörstrand, ca. 1955. Various handled ewers and vases.
Designed by Gunnar Nylund. A popular design theme in
Scandinavian ceramics is the handled vase or ewer.
Nylund was a master of this form, and the pieces
pictured here are a good cross section of his work.
$200-400.

Top: Rörstrand, ca. 1945. White/ivory matte glaze dishes. 4 inches high. Designed by Gunnar Nylund. $200-300.

Bottom: Rörstrand, ca. 1955. Earthy brown/green matte glaze vase. Designed by Gunnar Nylund. *Courtesy of Target Gallery, London.* $200-300.

Left: Rörstrand, ca. 1955. Slate blue matte glaze long necked vase. 8.75 inches high. Designed by Gunnar Nylund. $400-500.

Right: Rörstrand, ca. 1950. Blue gloss glaze cylindrical vase with ribbed body. 8 inches high. Designed by Gunnar Nylund. $100-200.

Left: Rörstrand, ca. 1950. Green matte glaze vase with subtle in-glaze decoration. 6 inches high. Designed by Gunnar Nylund. $250-350.

Top right: Rörstrand, ca. 1950. Brown matte glaze Chamotte body "Igloo" vase. Designed by Gunnar Nylund. *Courtesy of Antigo Decorative Arts, London.* $100-200.

Bottom right: Rörstrand, ca. 1950. Blue/green matte glaze bulbous shape vase. 5.75 inches high. Designed and made by Gunnar Nylund. *Courtesy of Kenneth Stern.* $250-350.

Top left: Rörstrand, ca. 1955. Blue and white striped matte glaze vase. 4.25. inches high. Designed and made by Gunnar Nylund. *Courtesy of Kenneth Stern.* $250-350.

Top right: Rörstrand, ca. 1955. Green semi-matte glaze squat shaped vase. 5.75 inches high. Designed and made by Gunnar Nylund. *Courtesy of Kenneth Stern.* $200-300.

Bottom left: Rörstrand, ca. 1955. Nylund mark typical of the 1950s with Nylund's initials and the Rörstrand three crown mark.

Bottom right: Rörstrand, ca. 1940. Early Nylund mark with the Rörstrand crowns.

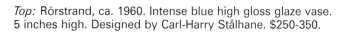

Top: Rörstrand, ca. 1960. Intense blue high gloss glaze vase. 5 inches high. Designed by Carl-Harry Stålhane. $250-350.

Bottom left & right: Rörstrand, ca. 1955. Two handled vases or ewers, one in cobalt blue matte glaze, the other in mottled beige and brown glaze flecked with green. Designed by Carl-Harry Stålhane. *Courtesy of Target Gallery, London.* $300-500.

Top: Rörstrand, ca. 1955. Small spherical vase in blue and gray shaded matte glaze. 2.5 inches high. Designed by Carl-Harry Stålhane. $250-350.

Bottom: Rörstrand, ca. 1955. Large shallow bowl or charger, in a spectacular blue matte glaze flecked with yellow and green. 18 in. diameter. Designed by Carl-Harry Stålhane. *Courtesy of Target Gallery, London.* $1000-1200.

Left: Rörstrand, ca. 1960. Unusual chalice-shaped footed bowl in ivory glaze with geometric design. Designed by Carl-Harry Stålhane. *Courtesy of Target Gallery, London.* $1000-1400.

Bottom right: Rörstrand, ca. 1955. Chocolate brown matte glaze egg shaped vase. 4 inches high. Designed by Carl-Harry Stålhane. *Courtesy of Target Gallery, London.* $300-400.

Top: Rörstrand, ca. 1955. Charcoal color matte glaze vase. 6.5 inches high. Designed by Carl-Harry Stålhane. *Courtesy of Target Gallery, London.* $300-400.

Center: Rörstrand, ca. 1955. Mottled gray and ivory matte glaze dish. Designed by Carl-Harry Stålhane. *Courtesy of Target Gallery, London.* $250-350.

Bottom: Rörstrand, ca. 1960. Very unusual flaring cylindrical vase in yellow matte glaze with shades of green, brown and red mixed in. 5.5 inches high. Designed by Carl-Harry Stålhane. $300-400.

Top: Rörstrand, ca. 1966. Rare hand glazed dish in shades of green blue and gun metal glaze. The underside illustrating how the glaze has dripped down the sides of the dish. 6 inches in diameter. Designed glazed and made by Carl-Harry Stålhane. Most of the work by Stålhane for Rörstrand consists of pieces he designed, but which were executed by others under his direction. A very few pieces, such as this one are found signed with a complete signature rather with initials. These pieces are sometimes also dated. $600-700.

Bottom: Rörstrand, ca. 1960. Green and brown shaded semi-matte glaze egg shaped vase. 4 inches high. Designed by Carl-Harry Stålhane. $150-250.

Left: Rörstrand, ca. 1953. Lustrous green matte glaze "hyancinth" vase. 8 inches high. Biomorphic shapes such as this, combined with fine glazes which, while muted in color, have incredible depth, epitomize the post-war Scandinavian style. Designed by Carl-Harry Stålhane. $400-500.

Right: Rörstrand, ca. 1955. Brown and gunmetal gray matte and gloss glaze vase. 6 inches high. Designed and glazed by Carl-Harry Stålhane. This piece is marked with Stålhane's initials and "Studio" mark. $850-1000.

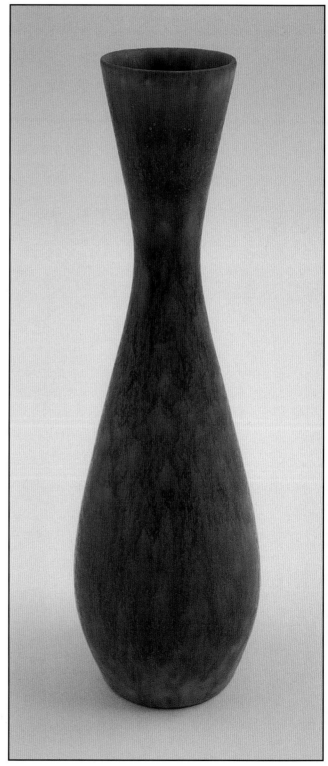

Top left: Rörstrand, ca. 1955. Two vases in a primitive ivory and gray matte glaze. Designed by Carl-Harry Stålhane. $250-400.

Center left: Rörstrand, ca. 1955. Two miniature vases in brown matte glaze. 2.5 inches high. Designed by Carl-Harry Stålhane. $200-300.

Bottom right: Rörstrand, ca. 1955. Blue with yellow/beige streaks matte glaze vase. 6.75 inches high. Designed by Carl-Harry Stålhane. $350-500.

Left: Rörstrand, ca. 1955. Cream colored matted glaze vase. 7.75 inches high. Designed by Carl-Harry Stålhane. $350-450.

Upper right: Rörstrand, ca. 1960. Blue and charcoal high gloss glaze bowl with underglaze incised design. 4.5 inches high. Designed by Carl-Harry Stålhane. $150-250.

Lower right: Rörstrand, ca. 1955. Blue and black high gloss glaze vase. 4.25 inches high. Designed by Carl-Harry Stålhane. *Courtesy of Kenneth Stern.* $250-350.

Top: Rörstrand, ca. 1965. Multi colored high gloss glaze vase. 4.5 inches high. Designed by Carl-Harry Stålhane. *Courtesy of Kenneth Stern.* $200-300.

Bottom: Rörstrand, ca. 1953. Yellow oil spot matte glaze spherical vase. 3.25 inches high. Designed and glazed by Carl-Harry Stålhane. $500-600.

Top left: Rörstrand, ca. 1960. Brown matte glaze vase. 6 inches high. Designed by Carl-Harry Stålhane. $250-350.

Top right: Rörstrand, ca. 1955. Cream color matte glaze hourglass vase with green vertical line design. 7 inches high. Designed by Carl-Harry Stålhane. $200-300.

Bottom left: : Rörstrand, ca. 1967. Example of Stålhane's signature mark, with date.

Bottom right: Rörstrand, ca. 1960. Example of typical Stålhane initial mark.

Top left: Rörstrand, ca. 1960. Blue high gloss glaze covered jar with under-glaze decoration. 5 inches high. Designed by Hertha Bengston. *Courtesy of Jackson's Twentieth Century Design, Stockholm.* $75-150.

Top right & bottom: Rörstrand, ca. 1960. Blue glaze coffee pot and bowl with underglaze design, from the "Blå Eld" (Blue Fire) series. Designed by Hertha Bengston in 1949, and in production from 1951 to 1971. Most pieces found are blue, however this series was also produced in red and gray. *Courtesy of Jackson's Twentieth Century Design, Stockholm.* $150-250.

Top: Rörstrand, ca. 1965. Blue glaze over Chamotte body vase. 7 inches high. Designed by Inger Persson. $100-175.

Center: Rörstrand, ca. 1970. Tea pot in bright orange glaze, shading to red on the lid. Designed by Inger Persson, this is part of the "Pop" series, and was produced in many bold colors. $300-400.

Bottom: Rörstrand, ca. 1960. Gunmetal blue matte glaze spherical vase. 5.5 inches high. Designed by Inger Persson. *Courtesy of Kenneth Stern.* $250-350.

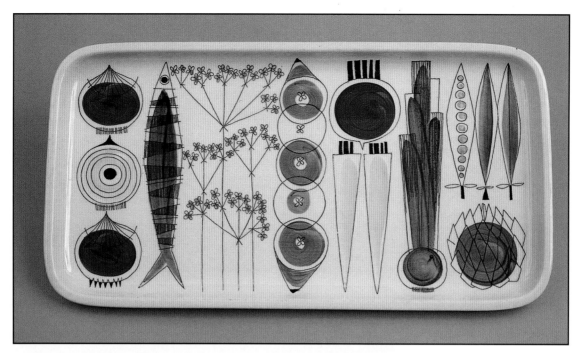

Bottom: Rörstrand, ca. 1965. White glaze coffee pot with incised design. $50-75.

Top: Rörstrand, ca. 1960. Serving tray in the "Picknick" series. Designed by Marianne Westman. $35-50.

Center: Rörstrand, ca. 1955. Two plates from the "Ark" series. $35-50.

Top left; Tobo, ca. 1950s. Dark brown matte glaze vase with high shoulder. 6.25 inches high. Designed, glazed, and thrown by Erich and Ingrid Triller. *Courtesy of Kenneth Stern.* $750-850.

Bottom left & right: Tobo, ca. 1950s. Brown matte glaze bottle form vases. The glaze with subtle mottling. Both approximately 5 inches high. Designed, glazed, and thrown by Erich and Ingrid Triller. *Courtesy of Kenneth Stern.* $400-500.

Top: Tobo, ca. 1950s. Light brown matte glaze narrow mouth vase. 4.25 inches high. Designed, glazed, and thrown by Erich and Ingrid Triller. *Courtesy of Kenneth Stern.* $400-500.

Bottom: Tobo, ca. 1950s. Three vases in subtle brown matte glazes. The cylindrical shapes are typical of Tobo, and demonstrate the level of technical achievement found in all Tobo pieces. All pieces were hand thrown by the Trillers. Combining this with their quest for perfection means that the number of pieces produced were limited compared with the output of the larger companies. 4.5 to 5.5 inches high. *Courtesy of Kenneth Stern.* $400-600.

Top right: Tobo, ca. 1950s. Dark, intense cobalt blue matte glaze vase. 3.75 inches high. While earth tones predominate in Scandinavian ceramics, blues were also very popular. Difficult to produce, when done properly, as in this example, they are magnificent. Designed, glazed, and thrown by Erich and Ingrid Triller. *Courtesy of Kenneth Stern.* $650-850.

Top left: Tobo, ca. 1950s. Brown mottled matte glaze bulbous form vase. 3 inches high. Designed, glazed, and thrown by Erich and Ingrid Triller. *Courtesy of Kenneth Stern.* $400-500.

Bottom: Tobo, ca. 1950s. Mustard yellow matte glaze wide mouth vase. 4 inches high. Designed, glazed, and thrown by Erich and Ingrid Triller. *Courtesy of Kenneth Stern.* $500-600.

Top left: Tobo, ca. 1950s. Brown hare fur glaze vase. 5 inches high. This vase presents a good example of a combination of classical shape and glaze. Designed, glazed, and thrown by Erich and Ingrid Triller. *Courtesy of Kenneth Stern.* $500-600.

Top right: Tobo, ca. 1950s. White matte glaze narrow mouth glaze. 6 inches high. Unlike the white glaze found on Saxbo pottery, which has a cream to beige undercolor, this glaze is intensely white. Designed, glazed, and thrown by Erich and Ingrid Triller. *Courtesy of Kenneth Stern.* $500-600.

Bottom: Tobo, ca. 1950s. Green/blue matte glaze narrow mouth vase. 6 inches high. Another beautiful example of the quality of the glazes produced by the Trillers on a timeless classical shape. *Courtesy of Kenneth Stern.* $750-1000.

Left: Tobo, ca. 1950s. Large light red/brown matte glaze vase. 9.75 inches high. Designed, glazed, and thrown by Erich and Ingrid Triller. Another example of why Tobo pieces were so eagerly collected by King Gustavus VI Adolphus of Sweden. *Courtesy of Kenneth Stern.* $1000-1200.

Top right: Tobo, ca. 1960. Shopmark with Triller signature.

Center right: Upsala-Ekeby, ca. 1950. Blue high gloss glaze egg shaped vase. 3.5 inches high. Designed by Vicke Lindstrand. Best known for his glass designs at both Orrefors and Kosta, Lindstrand also designed ceramics for a time and was at Upsala-Ekeby from 1936 to 1950. $75-125.

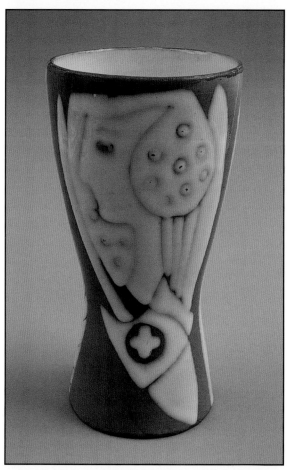

Top: Upsala-Ekeby, ca. 1955. Blue, black and white glaze design bowl. 16 in. length. $75-125.

Bottom: Upsala-Ekeby, ca.1950. Hourglass shaped vase with white glaze figural design. 11 inches high. Designed by Anna Lisa Thompson. $100-150.

Top: Upsala-Ekeby, ca. 1960. Platter in muted gray/blue glaze. $75-125.

Bottom: Upsala-Ekeby, ca. 1965. Colorful plate with undersea theme decoration. $50-100.

113

Top left: Hand painted tin-glazed bowl with colorful stylized flower design, ca. 1950. 5.25 inches in diameter. $50-75.

Top right: Hand painted sculptural wall plaque, ca. 1965. $50-75.

Bottom right: Stoneware vase with swirling glaze decoration, ca. 1950. $50-75.

Top: Ekeby, ca. 1950. Spherical gray high glaze vase. $75-125.

Center: Stoneware vase ca. 1960. 6 inches high. Marked THO NITTSJÖ. $50-75.

Bottom: Interesting closed vase in mottled brown semi-matte glaze, designed by Yngve Blixt. $200-300.

Iceland

Iceland did not produce ceramics until the 1920s, when Gudmundur Einarsson found numerous types of native clay to use for production. Ragnar Kjartansson a student of Einarsson took over, and, with the help of a friend, opened Glit Ceramics. Glit is best known for its unique clay, a mixture of volcanic basalt lava rock and clay. This creates a unique texture and temperature stability for use with hot or cold food and drink. Ragnar Kjartansson, in addition to making vases and bowls, also created ceramic murals with tiles. Glit also hired other artists, some working in traditional clay. One of note is Steinun Marteinsdottir, whose work has a more feminine and sculptural style.

Colorful ceramic plaque, ca. 1960. 7.25 inches long, marked Kjarval Lokken. $50-100.

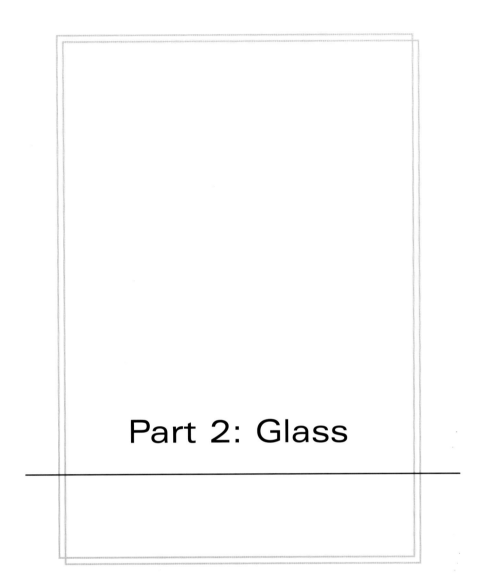

Part 2: Glass

Denmark

Denmark has fewer glassworks than the other Scandinavian countries, due to a lack of forest to fuel the furnaces. From the end of World War II to the 1970s the firms of Kastrup and Holmegaard dominated the art and utilitarian glass industry in Denmark.

The Danish Royal Family founded Holmegaard in 1825. Its initial purpose was to produce utilitarian glass, but in time Holmegaard began making art glass in the prevailing European style of the 19th Century. It was not until the 1920s that Holmegaard concentrated on art glass as a priority.

In 1925 Jacob Bang was appointed staff designer, bringing Art Deco design to the output of Holmegaard. He utilized simple, bold forms with wheel cut decoration. In 1942 Per Lütken succeeded Jacob Bang as designer. Lütken's designs are usually free flowing organic forms in soft shapes, often in a single blue-gray smoky tint. Michael Bang, who is the son of Jacob Bang, joined Holmegaard in 1968 giving the firm's production a new look of simple shapes in clear and colored glass. In 1965 Holmegaard merged with Kastrup to become Kastrup-Holmegaard. In 1975 it was acquired by Royal Copenhagen.

Kastrup was founded in 1847 to make bottles. It was under the same management as Holmegaard until 1873, when it was sold. Joining with some small glasshouses nearby, Kastrup produced industrial glass. In 1957 Jacob Bang (formerly with Holmegaard) became art director and in 1957 he was joined by Grethe Meyer and Ibi Trier Morch.

It is interesting to note that Bang, Meyer, and Morch were all trained to be architects.

At Kastrup they designed simple yet elegant glassware with emphasis on form and function.

Holmegaard, ca. 1955. Blue glass candlesticks, designed by Per Lütken. Signed PL 18373. $25-50.

Left: Holmegaard, ca. 1958. Smoke gray decanter and four glasses, designed by Per Lütken. $150-250.

Two at right: Holmegaard, ca. 1958. Two smoke colored glass vases, designed by Per Lütken. $100-200.

Finland

The origins of glassmaking in Finland date back to the seventeenth century but the beginnings of the modern Finnish glass industry can be traced to the establishment of Nuutajärvi in 1793, Iittala in 1881, Karhula in 1888, and Riihimaki in 1910. Compared to Sweden, the development of art glass in Finland was late. Early attempts by Nuutajärvi and Riihimaki, in the 1920s, to create interest in Finnish art glass were not particularly successful. However, by the early 1930s, led by Alvar and Aino Aalto, Finnish modernism began to take a leading role in the modern movement. The Savoy vase designed by Alvar Aalto for the Savoy restaurant in Helsinki has become one of the icons of modern design and is still in production today.

Iittala, ca. 1958. Two "Kantarelli" (Chanterelle) vases, designed by Tapio Wirkkala. The "Kantarelli" vase series, originally designed for the 1951 Milan Tirienniale, has become one of the most recognized symbols of Finnish art glass. Following the success of the original 50 hand produced pieces, several versions were put into production by Iittala. The illustrated pieces are models 3282 (short) and 3551 (tall). 4.5 and 12 inches high. $150-300.

Following the end of the World War II, Finland burst on the international design scene. The Finns won many prizes at the 1954 and 1957 Milan Trienniales. Designers such as Gunnel Nyman, Kaj Franck, Tapio Wirkkala, Saara Hopea, Nanny Still, Timo Sarpaneva, and Oiva Toikka dominated the period from the mid-century through the 1980s. As with the ceramics companies, mergers have resulted in all the companies being combined. In 1988 Iittala and Nuutajärvi merged. In 1990 they were acquired by Hackman and, eventually, by Designor Oy.

Mid-century glass design at Iittala can be summarized in two words, Wirkkala and Sarpaneva. Tapio Wirkkala joined Iittala in 1946, and Timo Sarpaneva in 1950. Between them they created some of the most original and exciting designs in international art glass. Sarpaneva, in particular, created objects, rather than vases or bowls. While some of his pieces, such as "Orkidea," could be used as a vase they functioned primarily as objects to be admired for their form rather than function. Sarpaneva used colored glass to create a subtle feeling, as in his colored glass disks, or by combining cool blue and gray shading with subtle shapes, as in his *i* series decanters. Wirkkala's work in glass is consistent with his overall design philosophy of creating from nature. His designs are generally drawn from the Lapland countryside, and forests of northern Finland. One of his most popular and recognizable designs is the "Kanttarelli" vase, first created in 1947. The first pieces were created in a limited run of fifty, and then a second group of fifty. It was feared that they would be too expensive and difficult to produce, but a simplification of the design proved it could be done. The design was a mainstay of the Iittala catalog through the 1960s. In addition to art glass, Wirkkala's designs were used for more utilitarian wares such as drinking glasses, and the ubiquitous Finlandia Vodka bottle. Wirkkala continued to design for Iittala until his death in 1985.

The designers at Nuutajärvi were no less influential or prolific than at Iittala. Gunnel Nyman, who died in 1948, produced vases with controlled bubbles in 1946, which remained in production for many years after her death. The "Calla" vase, shaped like a calla lily was also an icon of the 1950s. Kaj Franck joined Nuutajärvi in 1950. Along with Saara Hopea who joined the firm in 1952, they produced glass with clean simple shapes, usually in color. This emphasis on colored glass and pure simple almost liquid shapes differentiates the styles of Nuutajärvi from Iittala. Jaakko Niemi who was a master glassblower at Nuutajärvi also designed subtly shaped glass. Oiva Toikka, who came to Nuutajärvi in 1963 designed in a more pictorial style. His pieces were decorated in whimsical themes, such as his "Flora" series of bowls and vases, or animal or bird forms.

Iittala, ca. 1960. "Tree" vase, designed by Tapio Wirkkala. Wirkkala, arguably the designer who influenced post-war Finnish design to the greatest extent, took the forms found in nature as his models. This series of glass models itself after the trees found in the forests. Many of these pieces were formed in molds made from sculpted wooden forms. Model mark 3929. 7 inches high. $250-350.

Top: Iittala, ca. 1960. Four drinking glasses, designed by Tapio Wirkkala. *$25-50.*

Bottom: Iittala, ca. 1960. Two candlesticks, designed by Tapio Wirkkala. *$50-75.*

Top left: Iittala, ca. 1960. Frosted and smoke gray glass vase, designed by Tapio Wirkkala. Production model 3502. 6.25 inches high. *Courtesy of Kenneth Stern.* $600-800.

Top right: Iittala, ca. 1960. Footed violet colored glass bowl, designed by Tapio Wirkkala. 8 inches in diameter. Production model 3588. $300-400.

Bottom: Iittala, ca. 1960. Two colored glass vases, designed by Tapio Wirkkala. The color of these two pieces shades from blue to lavender. $300-500.

Left: Iittala, ca. 1956. Blue glass bud vase, designed by Tapio Wirkkala. Model 3299. 10 inches high. $175-275.

Right: Iittala, ca. 1959. Two blue vases, designed by Tapio Wirkkala. Production model 3586. 9.5 and 6 inches high. $150-300.

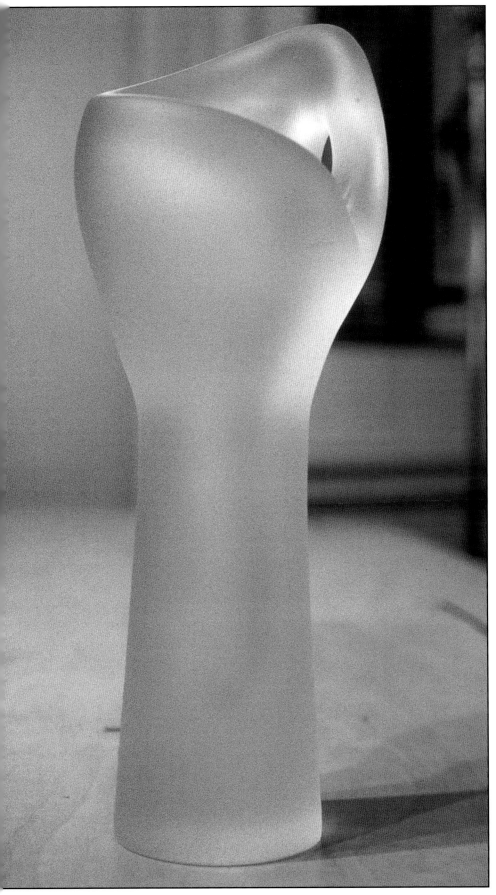

Left: Iittala, ca. 1955. Glass sand blasted sculpture from the "Pot Hole" or "Devils Churn" series, designed by Timo Sarpaneva. Model 3530. 11.75 inches high. Sarpaneva's approach to design was more biomorphic and sculptural than Wirkkala's. *Courtesy of Jackson's Twentieth Century Design.* $750-1000.

Right: Iittala, ca. 1960. Two sculptural pieces in the "Orkidea" (Orchid) series, designed by Timo Sarpaneva. In 1954 *House Beautiful* designated this "The Most Significant Object of the Year." Although they can be used as vases, they are described by Iittala as "Art Objects." Originally designed in 1954, they are still in limited production. Production model 3568. 10 and 5.5 inches high. These examples are from 1987. $300-500.

Left: Iittala, ca. 1959. Two i series decanters, designed by Timo Sarpaneva. The small round i-401 and tall i-403 are at the same time utilitarian and artistic. 11.5 and 6.5 inches high. $150-300.

Center right: Iittala, ca. 1959. i-400 decanter and glasses, designed by Timo Sarpaneva. 6.5 inches high. $150-250.

Bottom right: Iittala, ca. 1960. Cobalt blue decanter and glass, possibly designed by Timo Sarpaneva. 9 inches high. $100-200.

Top left: Iittala, ca. 1960. Blue bottle, designed by Timo Sarpaneva. Production model 3144. 8 inches high. $150-250.

Right: Iittala, ca. 1985. Black, white, and crystal cased glass "Claritas" series vase, designed by Timo Sarpaneva. 10.25 inches high. First produced in 1983, still in limited production. *Courtesy of Freeforms Ltd., London.* $750-1000.

Bottom left: Iittala, ca. 1960. Pink cut and frosted bowl, designed by Kaj Franck. Production model 3111. 4 inches in diameter. $300-400.

Top left: littala, ca. 1960. Heavy walled clear glass cylindrical vase with trapped air bubbles by Timo Sarpaneva. Production model 3144. 8 inches high. $200-300.

Top right and right: littala, ca. 1959. Two blown glass pieces incorporating trapped air bubbles, designed by Kaj Franck. $350-450.

Top left: littala, ca. 1970. Two clear glass candleholders. $25-50.

Top right: littala, ca. 1965. Finlandia style pitcher. $25-50.

Bottom: littala, ca. 1965. Glass dishes and bowl with impressed woodgrain design. $25-50.

Left: Nuutajärvi-Notsjö, ca. 1965. Large, blue glass two-piece sculptural centerpiece, designed by Oiva Toikka. This 19 in. high design can be used to hold small floating flowers or candles. *Courtesy of Auerbach and Maffia.* $750-1000.

Center right: Iittala, ca. 1960. Blue glass pitcher and glasses. $50-75.

Bottom right: Nuutajärvi-Notsjö, ca. 1966. Bowl in the "Flora" series, designed by Oiva Toikka. 9.5 inches in diameter. $100-150.

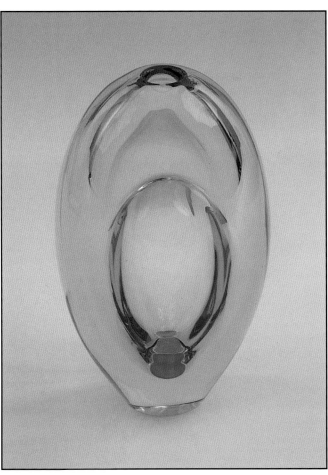

Nuutajärvi-Notsjö, ca. 1957. Spherical clear glass vase, designed and blown by Jaakko Niemi. 3.5 inches in diameter. Not as well known as Notsjö's other designers, Niemi was a master glass blower. He did, however, design few signed pieces. *Courtesy of Kenneth Stern.* $250-350

Nuutajärvi-Notsjö, ca. 1962. Cobalt blue blown and cut glass vase, designed and blown by Jaakko Niemi. 5.75 inches high. $200-300.

Nuutajärvi-Notsjö, ca. 1956. Clear glass "soap bubble" type vase, designed and blown by Jaakko Niemi. 6.5 inches high. $300-400.

Top two: Nuutajärvi-Notsjö, ca. 1955. Two decanters, and a vase possibly designed by Kaj Franck. $75-150.

Lower left: Nuutajärvi-Notsjö, ca. 1960. Two smoke and green glass vases designed by Kaj Franck. 4.25 inches high. $200-300.

Bottom right: Nuutajärvi-Notsjö, ca. 1955. Green glass bowl, designed by Kaj Franck. 7 inches high. $100-150.

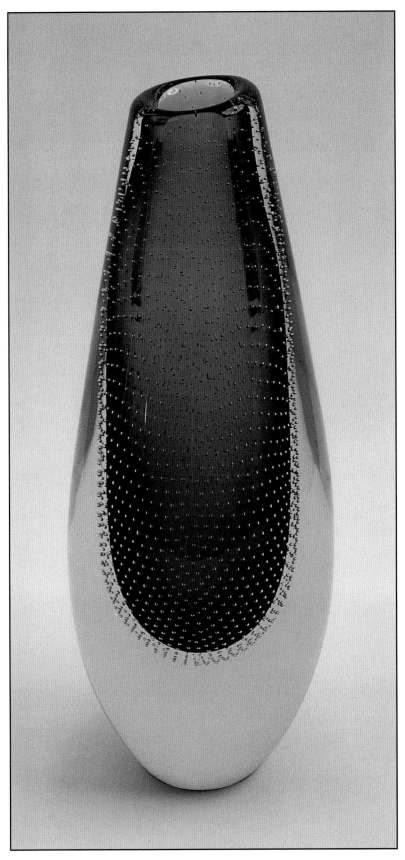

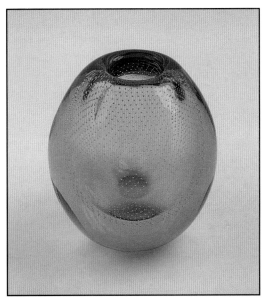

Left: Nuutajärvi-Notsjö, ca. 1959. Cased yellow glass vase with trapped spiral pattern air bubbles, designed by Gunnel Nyman. This style of vase, perfected by Nyman in the mid-1940s incorporated many of the elements which were to dominate Sandinavian art glass in the 1950s, heavy free-blown forms with soft colors and controlled air bubbles. Although Nyman died in 1948, her pieces were produced by Notsjö for many years (this example is dated 1959), and her work provided inspiration to many later artists. Model GN 26. 9.25 inches high. $350-500.

Top right: Nuutajärvi-Notsjö, ca. 1958. Cased clear, smoke and red glass vase, designed by Kaj Franck. 5.5 inches high. $350-500.

Bottom right: Nuutajärvi-Notsjö, ca. 1955. Clear spherical vase with trapped swirling air bubbles, designed by Gunnel Nyman. $200-300.

Sweden

Swedish glass production was centered in the Småland district of the country. In this small area many important glassworks produced some of the most beautiful art glass in the world. Two companies dominated the glass industry, Orrefors and Kosta. As with the ceramics industry they, along with smaller companies that they had earlier absorbed, are now part of the new Royal Scandinavia.

Orrefors has two beginnings: 1726, when a blast furnace and forge were founded on the site; and 1898 when Johan Samuelsson purchased the foundry. Lumbering was the primary industry at the site and, to utilize the excess wood, the manufacture of glass was begun with the firm of Orrefors Bruk AB. During the first quarter of the twentieth century glass in the art nouveau style predominated. This glass was similar to that produced in France by Gallé.

During the final years of World War I two designers who would have the most influence the future of Orrefors joined the firm: Simon Gate in 1916; and Edward Hald in 1917. Gate developed the Graal technique with glassblower Knut Bergkvist. In the next few years, production of glass in the Graal technique, as well as intricately designed wheel-engraved pieces predominated.

The next leap forward occurred about 1930, when Vicke Lindstrand joined the firm. During the 1930s the art glass produced by Orrefors reflected the Art Deco influence, with both Graal and cut designs. Lindstrand worked in the Graal and Ariel techniques, but also produced some of the most stylistic engraved and cut designs. He was later to produce most of the designs for the firm of Kosta, where he was the art director from 1950-1973.

Above: Orrefors, ca. 1957. Ariel vase in blue gray, designed by Edvin Öhrström, date mark 461F. 7 inches high. $1500-1700.

Right: Orrefors, ca. 1952. Three Ariel bowls in blue, red, and white, designed by Edvin Öhrström, date mark 1711E. 4.75 to 7 in. diameter. The Ariel technique as interpreted by Öhrström can be completely abstract, geometric, as it is here, or pictorial. $300-500.

Beginning in the 1930s, but especially in the late 1940s, following the World War II, and into the 1950s, several new designers joined the Orrefors. Edvin Öhrström, Sven Palmqvist, Nils Landberg, Ingeborg Lundin, and Gunnar Cyrén dominated production in the post war period.

Öhrström joined Orrefors in 1936, where his most important contribution was the introduction of the Ariel technique. Until his retirement in 1958 he produced heavy walled Ariel vases and bowls with intricate geometric designs, as well as images incorporating Nordic folklore.

Sven Palmqvist joined Orrefors in 1937. He contributed many new designs and techniques to Scandinavian art glass. The Kraka, Ravenna, and Fuga techniques dominated Orrefors glass of the 1950s. Palmqvist also produced wheel engraved designs. He remained at Orrefors until his death in 1984.

Nils Landberg joined Orrefors in 1925 as a student in the school of engraving, and then as a trainee designer. He is best known for the pure undecorated glass he produced in the 1940s and 1950s. The best known is probably the "Tulip" series of glasses from 1953, which appear so delicate one wonders how any could survive shipping. Landberg worked until 1972.

Ingeborg Lundin joined Orrefors in 1947. She represented the first of the next generation of artists to work at the factory, and she brought a new fresh style to her work. She worked in Ariel and engraved techniques, but may be best known for the simple elegant "Apple" vase of the 1950's. She left Orrefors in 1971.

Gunnar Cyrén joined Orrefors in 1959. In 1966 he won the prestigious Lunning prize for his work. His work combines themes from Nordic mythology with the Graal and engraved technique.

Above: Orrefors, ca. 1957. Ariel vase in blue and gold, designed by Edvin Öhrström, date mark 501F. 9.5 inches high. *Courtesy of Jackson's Twentieth Century Design, Stockholm.* $4000-5000.

Left: Orrefors, ca. 1975. Ariel vase in blue abstract pattern, designed by Ingeborg Lundin, date mark 212-E5. 8.5 inches in diameter. *Courtesy of Jackson's Twentieth Century Design, Stockholm.* $2000-2500.

Orrefors, ca. 1946. Kraka vase designed by Sven Palmqvist. 10 inches high. This is a very early example of the Kraka technique developed by Palmqvist. $1000-1200

Orrefors Art Glass Techniques

GRAAL
Developed in 1916, Graal takes its name from the story of the Holy Grail. The first color used in the process was dark red, perceived as blood or wine within the glass. The method of producing Graal is similar to cameo glass. Colored glass is drawn over a clear glass body while on the blowpipe. It is then cooled, and, if desired, a design can be cut into it.

ARIEL
This process, developed in the early 1930s by Bergkvist, Öhrström, and Lindstrand, takes its name from Ariel the air sprite in Shakespeare's Tempest. It is similar to the Graal technique in that one layer of glass is encased by another. In Ariel designs are placed between the layers by sandblasting. The trapped air forms the design. Typically layers of colored glass are incorporated in the design.

KRAKA
Palmqvist developed this process in 1944. It is produced by placing a wire mesh over a glass blank that is etched to form the design. When covered by an outer layer of glass, the tiny air bubbles are trapped. The name comes from a Nordic legend of a woman who was draped by a fish net.

RAVENNA
Inspired by mosaics in Ravenna, Italy, Palmqvist developed this technique in 1948. It is similar to Ariel, but uses powdered colored glass between the layers. The air entrapment is not as pronounced.

FUGA
Fuga bowls are formed by centrifugal force. Molten glass is poured into a spinning mold, and centrifugal force moves the glass around the mold. The final shape is formed by a plunger pushing into the mold.

Anders Koskull and Georg Bogislaus Staël von Holstein founded Kosta Glassworks in 1742. Through most of the eighteenth and nineteenth centuries, Kosta produced utilitarian glass such as drinking glasses and window glass. Like their rival, Orrefors, Kosta produced art glass in the Art Nouveau style at the beginning of the twentieth century. Gunnar Wennerberg was their first artist. Following the World War I, designs by Edvin Ollers were produced. These incorporated tinted glass decorated with delicate glass threads. The modern era of Kosta glass began with the arrival of Ellis Bergh in 1929. During the 1930s Bergh produced heavy undecorated glass, both clear and colored, which used the refractive quality of the glass itself as the predominant design element. Sven Erik Skawonius worked at Kosta during the 1930s producing sandblasted surrealistic designs in the glass.

In 1950, Vicke Lindstrand joined Kosta as head designer. Lindstrand had worked previously at both Orrefors and Upsala-Ekeby. For the most part, Lindstrand did not utilize the techniques used at Orrefors, but developed his own unique style. Vases with names such as "Trees in the Mist" and "Autumn" are examples. These vases incorporate colored glass strands between layers of clear glass. Lindstrand also produced wheel-engraved designs such as "Vanity," trapped bubble designs, and pure undecorated heavy walled cased glass vases and bowls.

Mona Morales-Schildt began working at Kosta in 1958. She worked with undecorated cased glass designs, but cut the vases to expose various layers of the design. These "Ventana" vases are some of the most original designs of the 1960's. She left Kosta in 1970.

In 1963 Kosta merged with two other glass companies, Åfors and Boda, to form the Åfors Group. In 1971 this was reorganized as Kosta Boda and also included Johansfors.

In the 1960s a new generation of designers joined Kosta. Ann and

Orrefors, ca. 1955. Kraka vase and bowls designed by Sven Palmqvist, date marks 342, 349. $400-650.

Top left: Orrefors, ca. 1965. Ravenna bowl in gold and blue designed by Sven Palmqvist, date mark 2676. 4.25 in. diameter. $650-750.

Top right: Orrefors, ca. 1965. Ravenna bowl in blue with gold highlights, designed by Sven Palmqvist, date mark 2665. 6.25 in. diameter. *Courtesy of Kenneth Stern.* $1200-1500.

Bottom: Orrefors, ca. 1958. Ravenna bowl in deep blue with gold swirl highlights, designed by Sven Palmqvist, date mark 1262. 7.25 inches long. $2000-2500.

Göran Wärff, Erik Höglund and Monica Backström, who started with Boda, Bertil Vallien and his wife, Ulrica Hydman-Vallien, and Signe Persson. With this influx of talent Kosta, and then Kosta Boda, took a new direction in design, becoming more daring and colorful. In 1975 Kosta Boda was acquired by Upsala-Ekeby and, in 1990, merged with Orrefors, ultimately becoming part of the Royal Scandinavia group in 1998.

Of the smaller glass companies in Sweden a few, such as Skruf, Åfors, Johansfors, and Strömbergshyttan, deserve mentioning. Skruf was founded in 1897. In 1953 Bengt Edenfalk joined the firm. He designed glass in a style called "Thalatta," which was similar to Ariel. His designs usually incorporate features from mythology or are purely stylistic. Åfors was founded in 1911. Their principle designer in the 1940s and 1950s was the Englishman Ernest Gordon, who worked in many styles, producing cut, cased and Ariel type art glass. Johansfors was founded in 1891 and produced primarily tableware. The designer Bengt Orup joined the company in 1952. Edvard and Gerda Strömberg formed Strömbergshyttan in 1933. Their glass is typically heavy walled and consists of vases and bowls in a clear blue tinted glass. As mentioned previously, these glass factories were eventually absorbed into the larger firms.

Top: Orrefors, ca. 1972. Ravenna vase in blue and lavender swirl pattern, designed by Sven Palmqvist, date mark 5452. 6 inches high. $850-1000.

Bottom: Orrefors, ca. 1955. Three "Fuga" bowls in blue, designed by Sven Palmqvist. 3 to 8 in. diameter. Fuga bowls were mass produced by Orrefors using a technique which spun the hot glass in a mold where it was shaped by centrifugal force. $100-200.

Top: Orrefors. Two "Colora" bowls in blue and orange designed by Sven Palmqvist. *Courtesy of Jackson's Twentieth Century Design, Stockholm.* $200-350.

Bottom: Orrefors, ca. 1956. Two smoke gray cased glass vases designed by Nils Landberg. Production mark NU 3538/3 and 3538/7. $200-300.

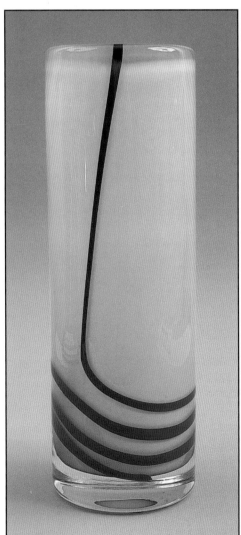

Far left: Orrefors, ca. 1957. Tall "Tulip" glass designed by Nils Landberg. 7.5 inches high. $250-350.

Top right: Orrefors, ca. 1968. Yellow swirl "Expo" bowl designed by Ingeborg Lundin, date mark 381-68. 10 inches in diameter. Orrefor's designers would occasionally produce special and unique "Expo" pieces which would be used to highlight the talents of a designer, to experiment with new techniques, or to display for special occasions. These pieces are marked "Expo" followed by a production/date code and the designer's name. $300-400.

Bottom: Orrefors, ca. 1973. Yellow and blue Expo vase designed by Olle Alberius. Date mark 253-73. 10.75 inches high. $500-750.

Left: Orrefors, ca. 1945. Large sandblast-finished, cut swirl design vase, designed by Vicke Lindstrand. Date/production mark LH 1457/3. Although Lindstrand left Orrefors in 1940, the company continued to release some of his designs. $300-400.

Right: Kosta, ca. 1955. Large wheel-engraved vase "In the Fishing Port," designed by Vicke Lindstrand. Date/production mark 42166. 10.25 inches high. $650-750.

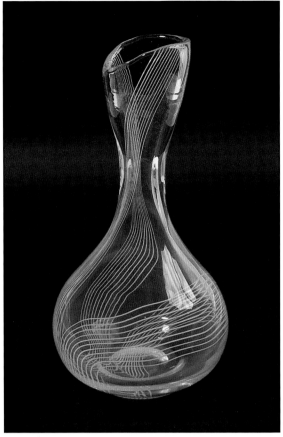

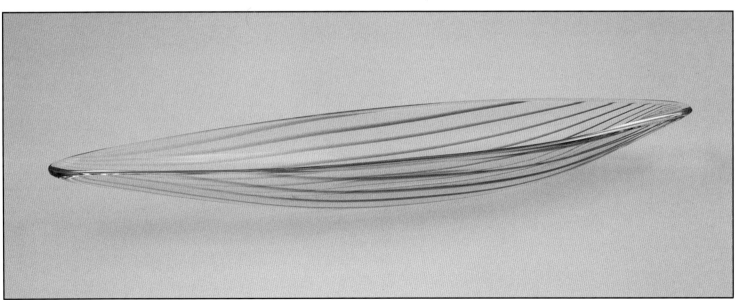

Top left: Kosta, ca. 1956. Wheel-engraved vase "Vanity," designed by Vicke Lindstrand. Production mark LG 180. 6.5 inches high. $250-350.

Top right: Kosta, ca. 1955. Vase "White Threads," designed by Vicke Lindstrand. Production mark LH 1155. 9 inches high. $200-300.

Bottom: Kosta, ca. 1959. Dish "Black Threads," designed by Vicke Lindstrand. Production mark LH 1387. 12.5 in long. $150-250.

Above left: Kosta, ca. 1957. Cased violet glass footed vase, designed by Vicke Lindstrand. Production mark LH 1567. 5 inches high. $150-250.

Above right: Kosta, ca. 1960. Cased glass bowl in red with white lines, designed by Vicke Lindstrand. Production mark L 1058. 3.5 inches high. *Courtesy of Kenneth Stern.* $200-300.

Bottom right: Kosta, ca. 1957. Cased violet/red and clear glass vase, designed by Vicke Lindstrand. Production mark LH 1444. 6 inches high. $200-300.

Kosta, ca. 1955. Two cased glass vases,
designed by Vicke Lindstrand. $250-350.

Left: Kosta, ca. 1956. Green decorated "Seaweed" vase, designed by Vicke Lindstrand. Signed Lindstrand 41803. 7.5 inches high. $300-500

Right: Kosta, ca. 1955. Multicolored decorated glass vase, designed by Vicke Lindstrand. Signed Lindstrand 1954. 8.5 inches high. Some of Lindstrand's most popular designs for Kosta were the series of vases which incorporated abstract colored glass decoration in a crystal body. Some of these designs were given names such as "Autumn," "Trees in the Mist," or "Black Grass." $1200-1500.

Top left: Kosta, ca. 1962. Prism cut, cased glass "Ventana" series vase in blue, green, and yellow, designed by Mona Morales-Schildt. The "Ventana" series consisted of prism cut colored glass vases. The cuts were designed to highlight the different colored glass layers. Signed Mona Schildt SS 172. 6.25 inches high. $500-750.

Above left: Kosta, ca. 1955. Unusual blue Ravenna-type bowl, designed by Vicke Lindstrand. Signed Lindstrand 56088. 7 inches in diameter. $500-600.

Bottom left: Kosta, ca. 1962. Prism cut blue glass "Ventana" vase designed by Mona Morales-Schildt. Production mark SS 202. 5 inches high. $400-500.

Kosta, ca. 1962. Four prism cut "Ventana" vases designed by Mona Morales-Schildt. *Courtesy of Jackson's Twentieth Century Design.* $500-750.

Above right: Boda, ca. 1975. Clear bowl with red glass band decoration, designed by Ulrica Hydman-Vallien. Signed Ulrica 57738. 8 inches in diameter. $150-250.

Above left: Kosta, ca. 1959. Blue cased glass vase, designed by Mona Morales-Schildt. 6 inches high. $250-350.

Bottom: Kosta, ca. 1970. Red and blue streaked glass decorated bowl, designed by Ann Wärff. Signed Wärff 77204. 6.5 inches in diameter. $250-350.

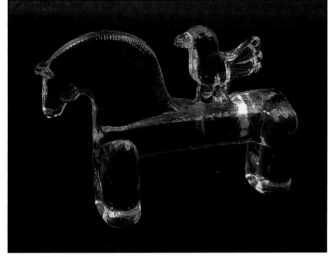

Above left: Boda, ca. 1965. Crystal molded horse and bird rider, designed by Erik Höglund. 6 inches long. $75-125.

Top right: Boda, ca. 1965. Blue glass molded plaque, designed by Erik Höglund. 6 inches long. $75-125.

Bottom: Boda, ca. 1975. Small "Network" bottle decorated with an impression from a screen, designed by Bertil Vallien. Signed Boda Artist B. Vallien 48012. 3.25 inches high. $75-125.

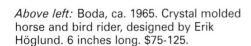

Above right: Boda, ca. 1976. White pillow-shaped vase with colored glass strand decoration, designed by Bertil Vallien. 6.5 inches high. $125-175.

Top left: Boda, ca. 1979. Blue and Black checker-board footed vase, designed by Bertil Vallien. 5 inches in diameter. *Courtesy of Kenneth Stern.* $200-300.

Bottom left: Kosta-Boda, ca. 1985. Clear vase decorated with a black glass spiral, designed by Bertil Vallien. Signed B. Vallien Kosta Boda 48414. 8 inches high. $150-250.

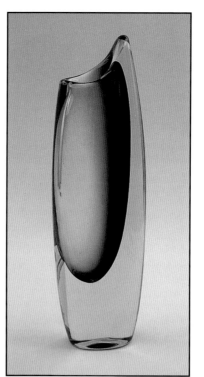

Strömbergshyttan, ca. 1955.
Several cased glass vases
designed by Gerda Strömberg.
$125-300.

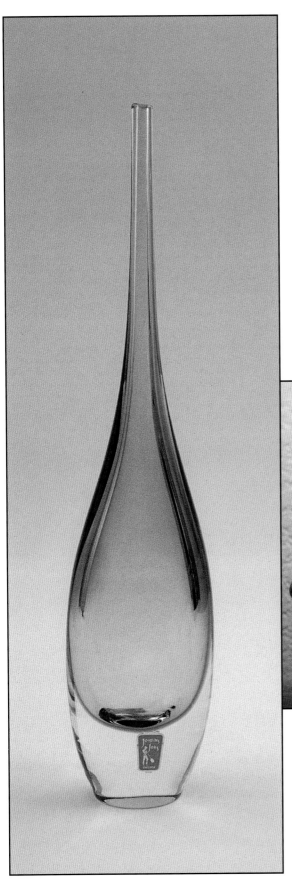

Top right: Skruf, ca. 1955. Large cobalt blue Thalatta vase, designed by Bengt Edenfalk. The Thalatta technique of Skruf is similar to Orrefor's Ariel, and is produced the same way, using trapped air to form the design. Signed Edenfalk Thalatta 7. 8.5 inches high. $1000-1200.

Lower two: Johansfors, ca. 1955. Two cased glass vases, designed by Bengt Orup. $100-200.

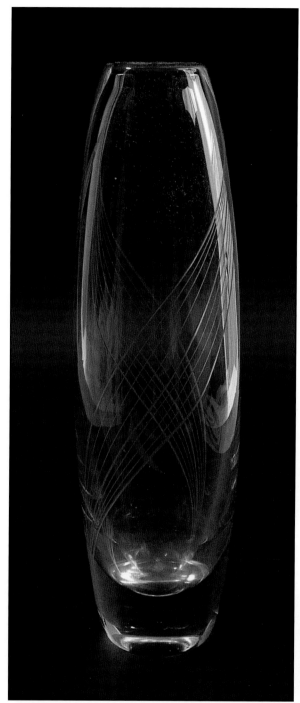

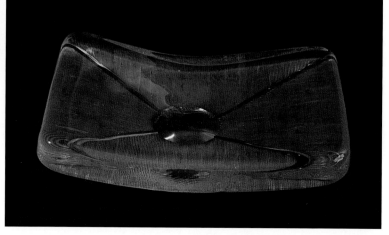

Top left: Åfors, ca. 1955. Wheel engraved spiral design vase, designed by Ernest Gordon. 9 inches high. *$150-250.*

Top right: Åfors, ca. 1955. Blue cased glass bottle-shaped vase, designed by Ernest Gordon. Signed Ernest Gordon GH 208. 10 inches high. $250-350.

Bottom right: Åfors, ca. 1955. Clear wheel cut bowl, designed by Ernest Gordon. Signed GS 1111 Ernest Gordon. 6.5 inches long. $150-250.

Several colored glass vases and pitchers, possibly Strömbershyttan and Johansfors, ca. 1955. $75-150.

Top: Reijmyre, ca. 1950.
Green cased glass vase,
designed by Monica Bratt. 6
inches high. $75-150

Center: Pukeberg, ca. 1960.
Glass knife rests. $35-50.

Bottom: Flygsfors, ca. 1950.
Two Coquille dishes, designed
by Paul Kedelv. 4 inches high.
Courtesy of Marcia Meirowitz.
$50-75.

Biographies of Artists

ALVAR AALTO (1898-1976) FINLAND

Aalto was an architect and a designer of furniture, glass, and lighting. In 1935 he founded the company Artek in Finland, which still produces his lighting and furniture designs. His Savoy vase of the 1930s is an icon of Finnish design. He designed the Finland Pavilion at the 1939 New York World's Fair and brought international attention to the aesthetic of Finnish modern design.

ARNE BANG (1901-197?) DENMARK

The brother of Jacob Bang, Arne produced ceramics in his own workshop beginning in the 1930s. He also worked at Holmegaard.

JACOB BANG (1899-1965) DENMARK

Bang worked as art director for Holmegaard beginning in 1928. He was responsible for the production of modern glass there. In the 1940s he was artistic director at Nymølle, where he worked until 1957.

GUNNAR CYRÉN (B.1931) SWEDEN

As one of latest generation of artists at Orrefors, Cyrén works in a playful style of glass design that features colorful scenes and characters. He was originally trained as a silversmith, and currently works in both media.

KAJ FRANCK (1911-1989) FINLAND

Franck is considered something of a renaissance man in the field of modern design, He is best known for his glass and ceramic designs for Arabia and Nuutajärvi-Notsjö. He originally studied furniture design, and also designed lighting. His glass and ceramics designs range from unique art pieces to everyday utilitarian wares. Many of his designs are still in production.

BERNDT FRIBERG (1899-1981) SWEDEN

Friberg spent almost his entire 50 odd year career at Gustavsberg. Starting as a thrower for Wilhelm Kåge in 1934, Friberg began his own career in 1944 at the Gustavsberg Studio, producing some of the most sought-after pottery. He created incredible glazes and forms and, unlike many of his contemporaries, he threw and glazed all of them himself.

FRIEDL HOLZER-KJELLBERG (1905-1993) AUSTRIA, FINLAND

Trained in Graz, Austria, Holzer-Kjellberg began working at Arabia in Finland in 1924. During the 1930s and 1940s she designed in the subtle style of Chinese Sung Dynasty pottery, using barium and oxblood type glazes. In the 1940s she perfected a style of porcelain known as rice porcelain. Made in large numbers for many years, this style of porcelain remains her most significant contribution.

NATHALIE KREBS (1895-1978) DENMARK

Krebs is best known as the founder of Saxbo. She began her career at Bing & Grøndahl, where she met Gunnar Nylund. The two of them left in 1929 to start their own ceramics studio. After Nylund left in 1930 she maintained the workshop and re-named it Saxbo. In 1932 Eva-Stæhr Nielsen joined Krebs, and together they produced pottery in the Chinese style, with Stæhr-Nielsen producing the shapes and Krebs the glazes.

NILS LANDBERG (1907-1991) SWEDEN

Beginning as a student in the Orrefors school of engraving, Landberg continued his career at Orrefors in the 1930s as an assistant to Edward Hald. During his 40 year career at Orrefors he produced engraved pieces as well as the delicately proportioned "Tulip" series of glasses.

STIG (SIGURD) LINDBERG (1916-1982) SWEDEN

Lindberg was one of the most influential Swedish ceramics designers of the post-war years. He began his career as an assistant to Wilhelm Kåge at Gustavsberg, and in 1949 became the artistic director at Gustavsberg. His designs include individual artist pieces, production decorative wares, represented by the many faience designs, and utilitarian wares, including flameproof dinnerware. His output also included plastics, and electronics. He will, however, be best remembered for his post-war ceramics.

VICKE (VIKTOR) LINDSTRAND (1904-1983) SWEDEN

In 1928 Lindstrand joined Orrefors. Along with Simon Gate and Edward Hald, Lindstrand developed the glass designs which were to make Orrefors glass world famous. He left in 1941 to work for the ceramics firm Upsala-Ekeby as the artistic director. In 1950, he became the artistic director at Kosta Glasbruk. During the 1950s Lindstrand's thick walled asymmetric glass designs at Kosta were some of the most successful of the period.

PER LINNEMANN-SCHMIDT (B.1912) DENMARK

Per Linnemann-Schmidt and his wife, Annelise (1918-1969), formed the ceramics studio named Palshus. They produced ceramics in the subtle Chinese Sung style popular in the 1950s. In the 1960s they produced ceramics with a rougher quality.

MONA (MONICA) MORALES-SCHILDT (B.1908) SWEDEN

Mona Schild began her career at Gustavsberg in 1935 working for Wilhelm Kåge. Prior to the outbreak of World War II she worked at Arabia in Finland. In 1957 she joined Kosta Glasbruk in Sweden where she designed elegant colored glass vases.

TOINI MUONA (1904-1987) FINLAND

Muona was hired by Arabia in 1931 and worked in the art department for the next 40 years. She is best known for her oxblood and copper glazes that were used on her famous reed vases of the 1940s.

JAAKKO NIEMI (B.1926) FINLAND

Master glassblower for Nuutajärvi-Notsjö during the 1950s and 1960s, he worked with Kaj Franck to produce art glass, as well as his own designs.

GUNNAR NYLUND (1904-1989) SWEDEN

Best known for his ceramics at Rörstrand, Nylund designed both ceramics and glass for many companies. He was originally trained as an architect and began his career at Bing & Grøndahl in 1926. He was co-founder of a ceramics company with Nathalie Krebs in 1929. He started working at Rörstrand in 1930. His output consisted primarily of rich, subtly glazed pottery typical of the post-war modern period. In the late 1950s Nylund also designed for Nymølle in Denmark, and Strombergshyttan glass in Sweden.

GUNNEL NYMAN (1909-1948) FINLAND

Her short career was marked by designs which became icons of modern design and inspired a generation of designers, in particular Tapio Wirkkala. Her "Calla" vases and heavy walled controlled bubble glass for Nuutajärvi-Notsjö, produced in 1946, remained in production for many years after her death.

EDVIN ÖHRSTRÖM (1906- 1994) SWEDEN

Originally trained as a sculptor, Öhrström is best known for the thick walled glass he designed for over 20 years at Orrefors. His Ariel technique vases are some of the most colorful and desirable pieces of Swedish glass. His designs range from purely geometric patterns to Nordic folktale inspired designs.

SVEN PALMQVIST (1906-1984) SWEDEN

Palmqvist learned his trade at the Orrefors engraving school in 1928. He was hired as an engraver at Orrefors in 1936. He is known as the developer of "Kraka," "Ravenna," and "Fuga" glass. He retired in 1972.

TIMO SARPANEVA (B.1926) FINLAND

Along with Tapio Wirkkala, Sarpaneva is one of the most celebrated Finnish designers of the modern era. His glass designs for Iittala, such as the "Orchid" vases and "Devils Churn" sculptures, are recognized as masterpieces of design. He has also designed textiles, flatware, and cooking pots.

CARL-HARRY STÅLHANE (1920-1990) SWEDEN

Stålhane began his career at Rörstrand in 1939. He was originally trained as a sculptor, and the pieces he designed during the next few years exhibit a sculptural quality. Subtle matte glazes were characteristic of his work in the 1950s. His later work is more rugged and individualistic. In 1973 he left Rörstrand to design and make pottery at his own studio.

AXEL SALTO (1889-1961) DENMARK

Salto began his career at Bing & Grøndahl in 1922. In 1933 he began a long collaboration with Royal Copenhagen. It was there that he produced his best known works until his death.

OIVA TOIKKA (B.1931) FINLAND

Toikka has worked at Arabia since 1956. He has also designed for Marimekko, and Rörstrand. In 1963 he became art director at Nuutajärvi-Notsjö.

ERICH (1898-1972) AND INGRID TRILLER (1905-1982) GERMANY/SWEDEN

In 1935 the Trillers established Tobo, a ceramics studio, where they produced very limited hand thrown and glazed ceramics. The hallmark of a Tobo piece is the perfection of the glaze and form. Tobo ceramics were a favorite of King Gustavus VI Adolfus of Sweden. Production ceased in 1972.

TAPIO WIRKKALA (1915-1985) FINLAND

Wirkkala is generally considered Finland's greatest, and most important post-war designer. In 1946 his "Kanterelli" vases for Iittala won him recognition. He designed bank notes for the Bank of Finland, decorative laminated wood trays and furniture, metalware, and the famous Puukko knife. He is also well-known for his porcelain designs for Rosenthal, and glass for Venini. Most of Wirkkala's designs take their inspiration from the forms of nature in his native Finland.

Bibliography

A *Treasury of Scandinavian Design*. Erik Zahle, Editor. Golden Press 1961.

Arabia. Kumela, C; K. Paatero; and K. Rissanen, Editors. Oy Wärtsilä AB Arabia 1987

Beer, Eileene Harrison. *Scandinavian Design; Objects of a Life Style*. Straus and Giroux 1975.

Design in Sweden. Lindkvist, Lennart, Editors. Swedish Society for Industrial Design 1972.

Design 1935 –1965 What Modern Was. Le Musée des Arts Décoratifs de Montréal Exhibition catalog. Harry N. Abrams 1991

Duncan, Alistair. *Orrefors Glass*. Antique Collectors Club 1995

Finnish Glass. Glass manufacturers' brochures from the 1950s. Riihimäki 1994.

Finnish Post War Glass 1945-1996. University of Sunderland Exhibition catalog 1996.

Hald, Arthur, and Sven Erik Skawonius. *Modern Swedish Design*. Nordisk Rotogravyr 1951.

Hård af Segerstad, Ulf. *Scandinavian Design*. Nordisk Rotogravyr 1961.

Hård af Segerstad, Ulf. *Berndt Friberg, Keramiker*. Nordisk Rotogravyr 1964.

Klyvare, Berndt, and Dag Widman. *Stig Lindberg: Swedish Artist and Designer*. Rabén & Sjögren 1963.

Kosta Glassworks Commemorating 250 Years of Craftsmanship. Margareta Artéus, Editor. Kosta Boda 1992.

Ricke, Helmut, and Ulrich Gronert. *Glas in Schweden 1915-1960*. Prestel-Verlag 1986.

Scandinavian Modern Design 1880-1980. Cooper-Hewitt Museum Exhibition catalog 1982. David Revere McFadden, Editor. Harry N. Abrams 1982.

Scandinavia Ceramics & Glass in the Twentieth Century. Victoria and Albert Museum catalog 1989. Jennifer Hawkins Opie, Editor. Rizzoli 1990.

Stennett_Willson, R. *The Beauty of Modern Glass*. The Studio Ltd. 1958.

Swedish Glass Factories, Production Catalogs 1915-1960. Helmut Ricke and Lars Thor, Editors. Prestel-Verlag 1987.